A TRUE WONDER

THE COMIC BOOK HERO WHO CHANGED EVERYTHING

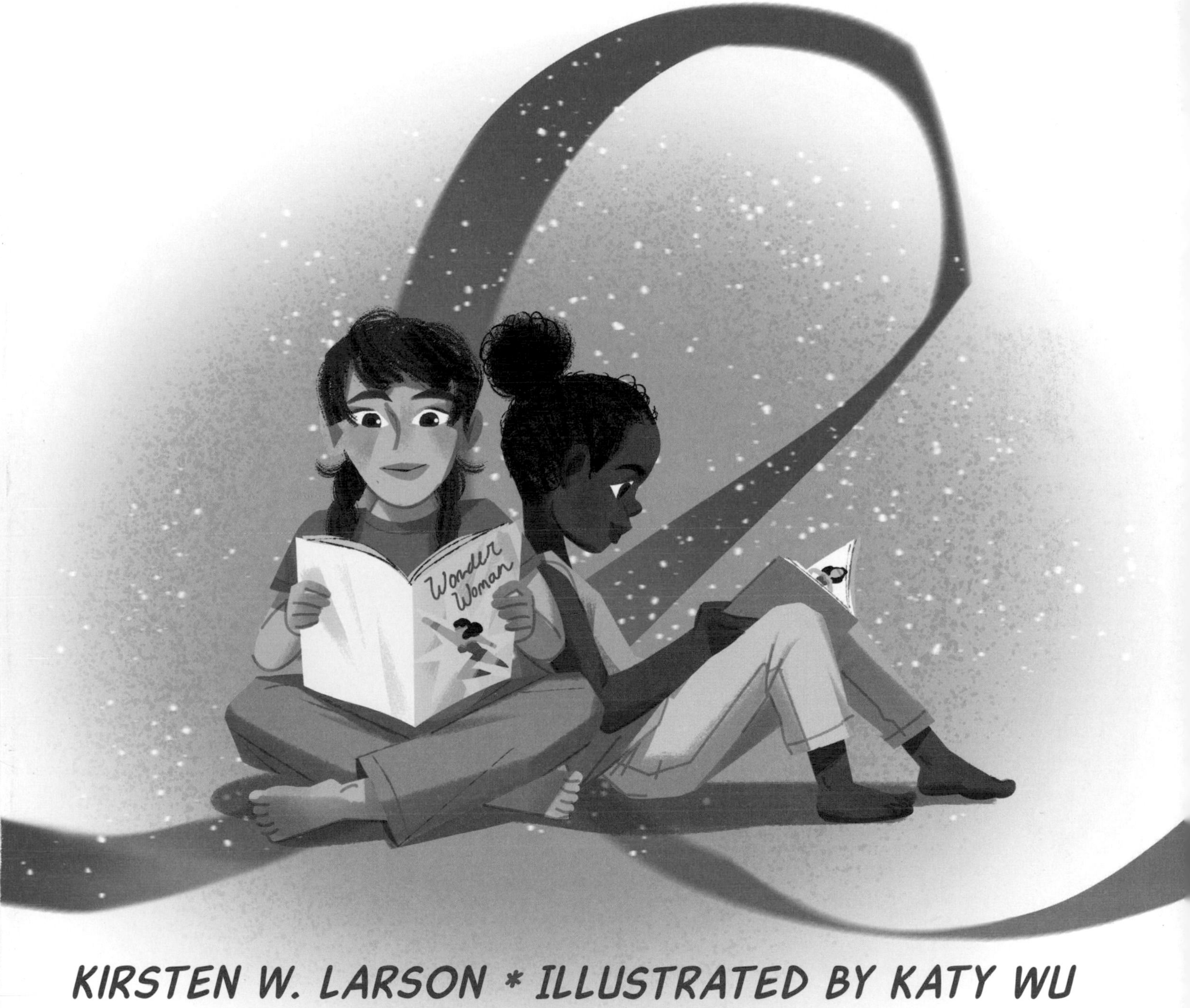
Wonder Woman

KIRSTEN W. LARSON * ILLUSTRATED BY KATY WU

CLARION BOOKS
Houghton Mifflin Harcourt
Boston New York

Clarion Books
3 Park Avenue
New York, New York 10016

Clarion Books is an imprint of Houghton Mifflin Harcourt Publishing Company.

hmhbooks.com

The illustrations in this book were done in Adobe Photoshop.
The text was set in Nobel.

Library of Congress Cataloging-in-Publication Data is available.
ISBN 978-0-358-23842-3

Manufactured in China
SCP 10 9 8 7 6 5 4 3 2 1
4500825596

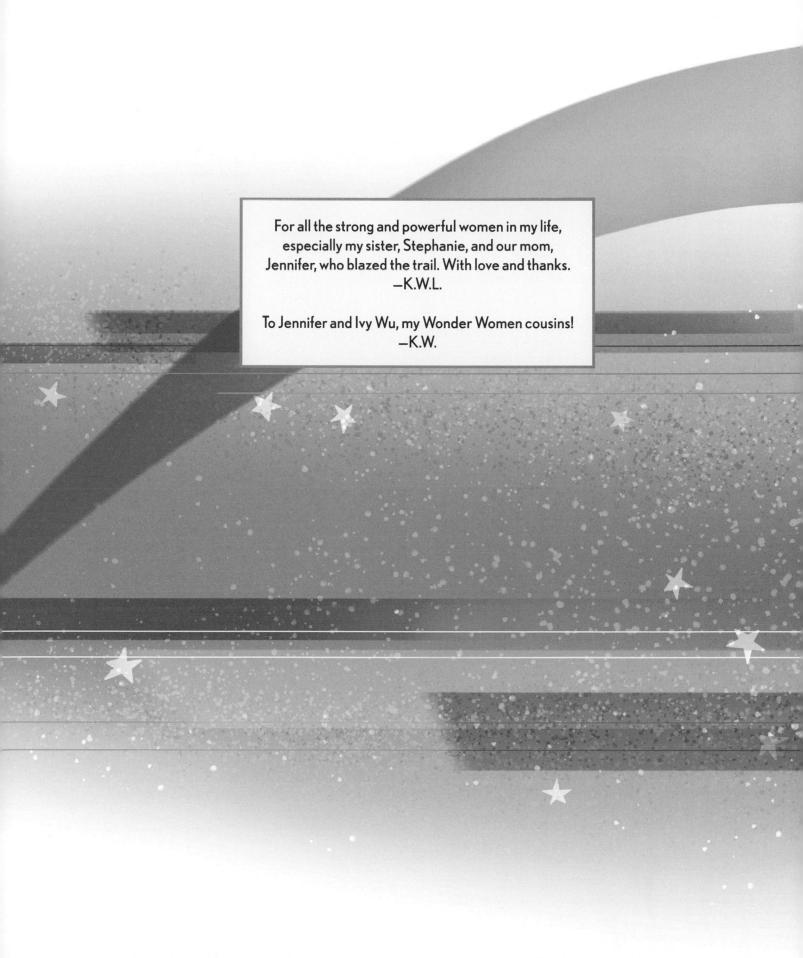

For all the strong and powerful women in my life,
especially my sister, Stephanie, and our mom,
Jennifer, who blazed the trail. With love and thanks.
—K.W.L.

To Jennifer and Ivy Wu, my Wonder Women cousins!
—K.W.

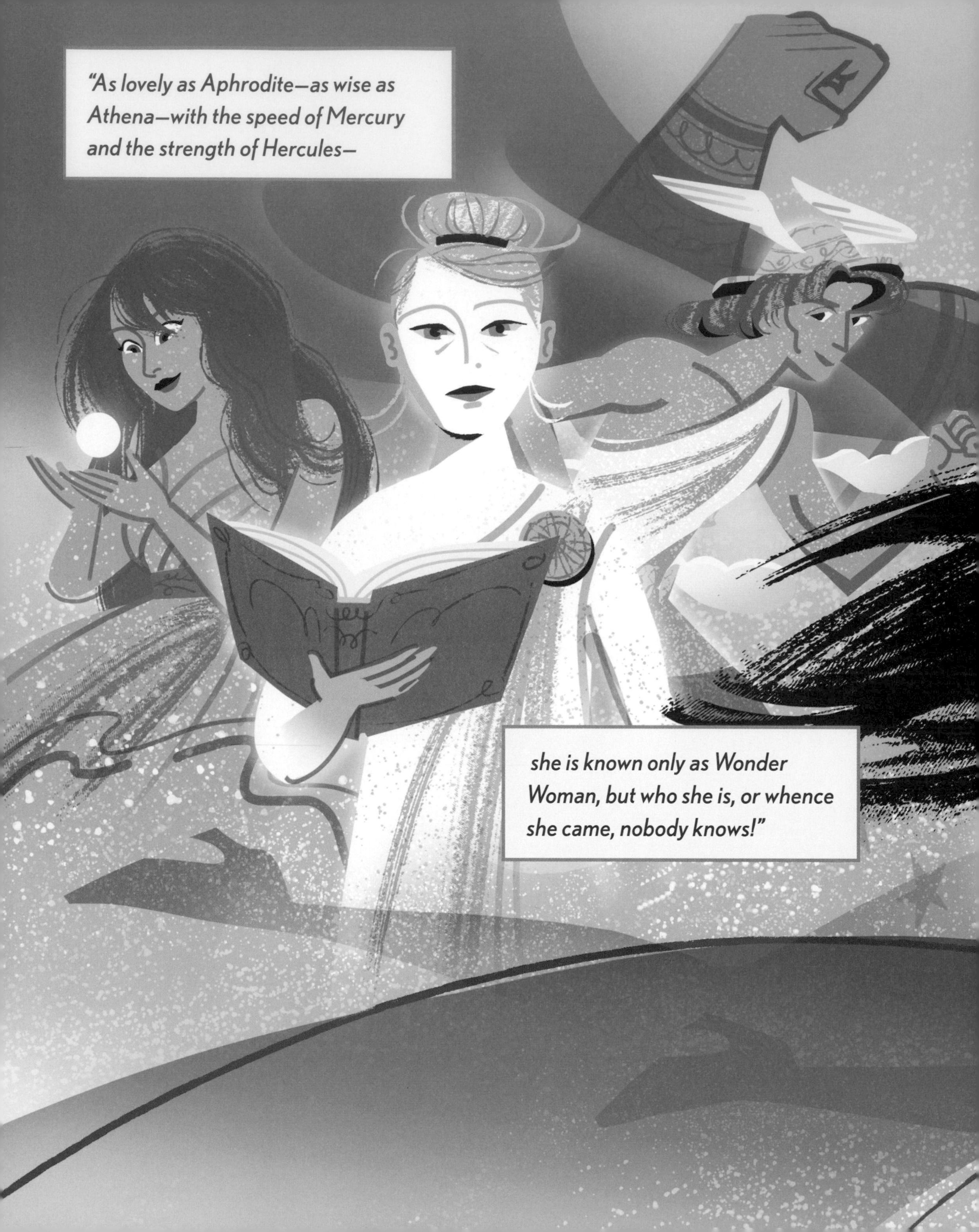
"As lovely as Aphrodite—as wise as Athena—with the speed of Mercury and the strength of Hercules—
she is known only as Wonder Woman, but who she is, or whence she came, nobody knows!"

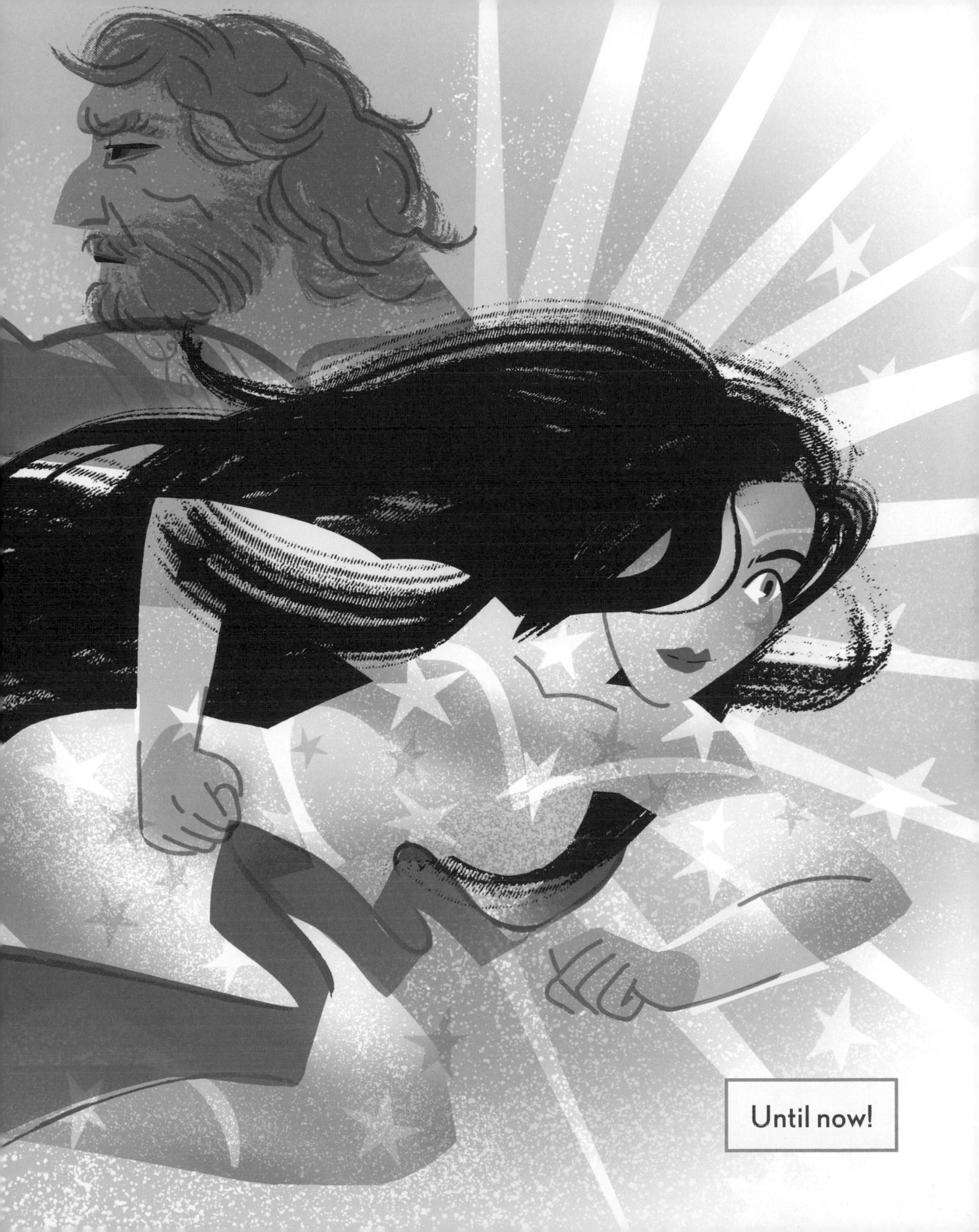
Until now!

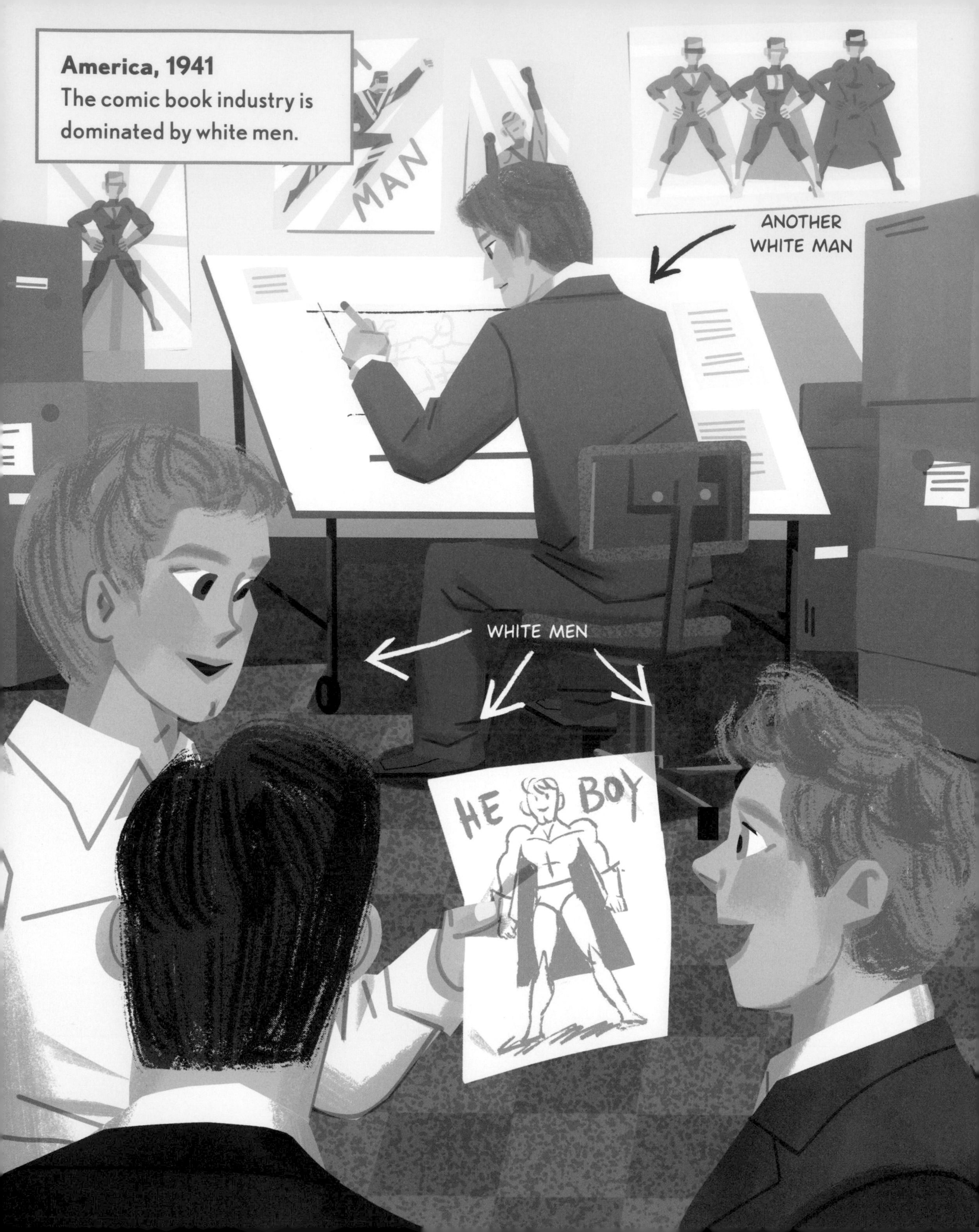
America, 1941
The comic book industry is dominated by white men.
MAN
ANOTHER WHITE MAN
WHITE MEN
HE BOY

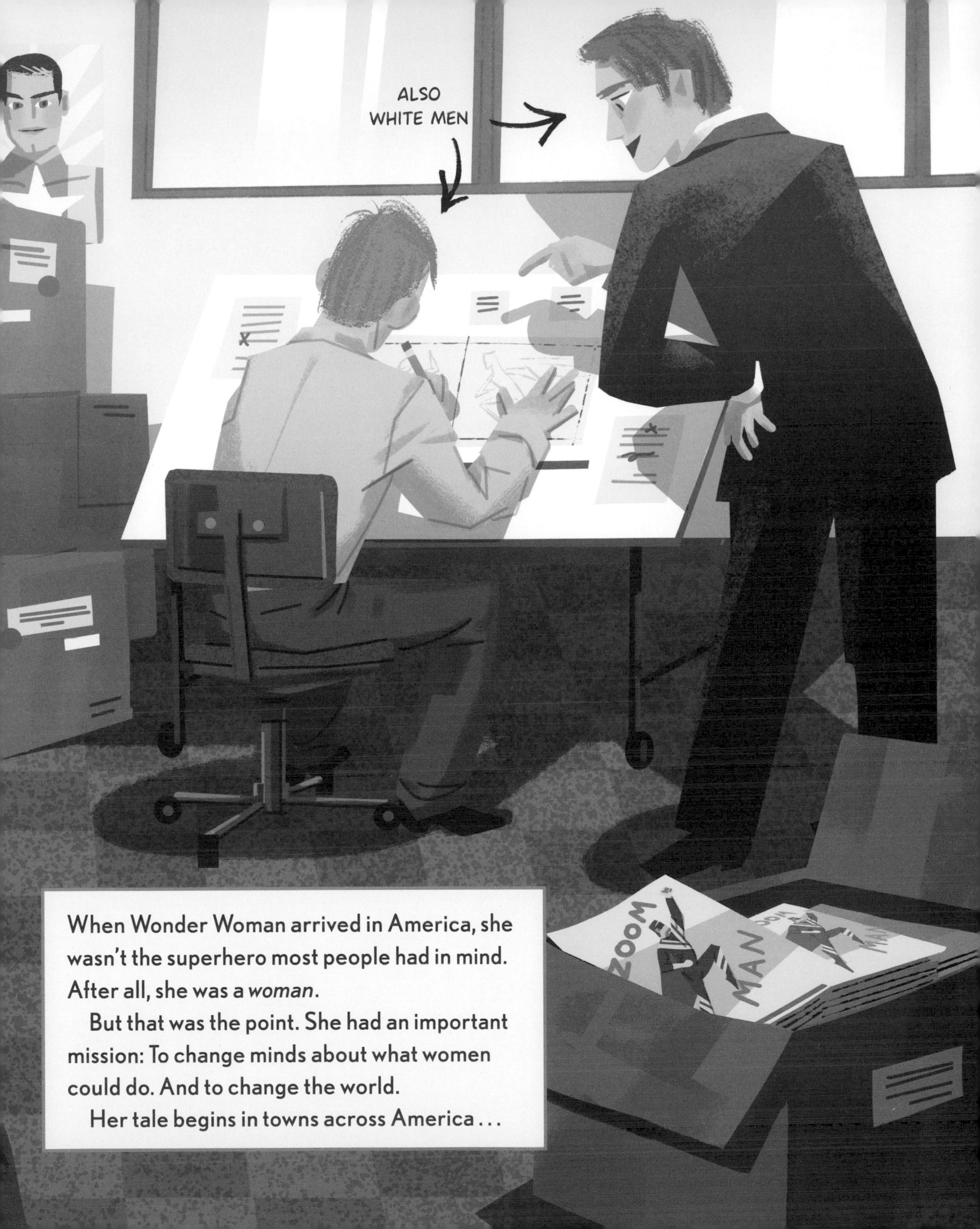
ALSO WHITE MEN
ZOOM MAN
ZOOM MAN

When Wonder Woman arrived in America, she wasn't the superhero most people had in mind. After all, she was a *woman*.

But that was the point. She had an important mission: To change minds about what women could do. And to change the world.

Her tale begins in towns across America . . .

Comic books were everywhere. Kids gobbled them up morning, noon, and way past bedtime.

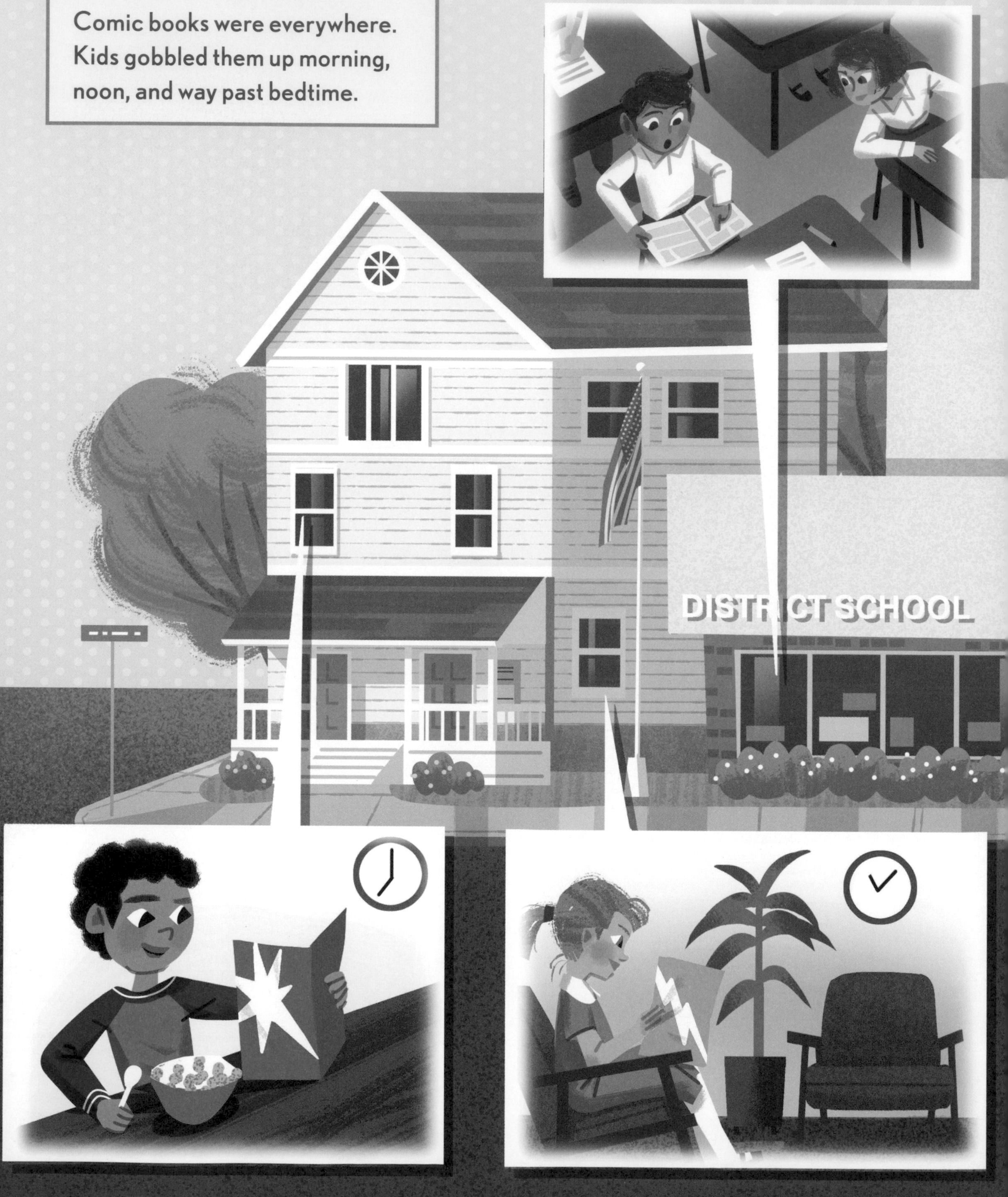
DISTRICT SCHOOL

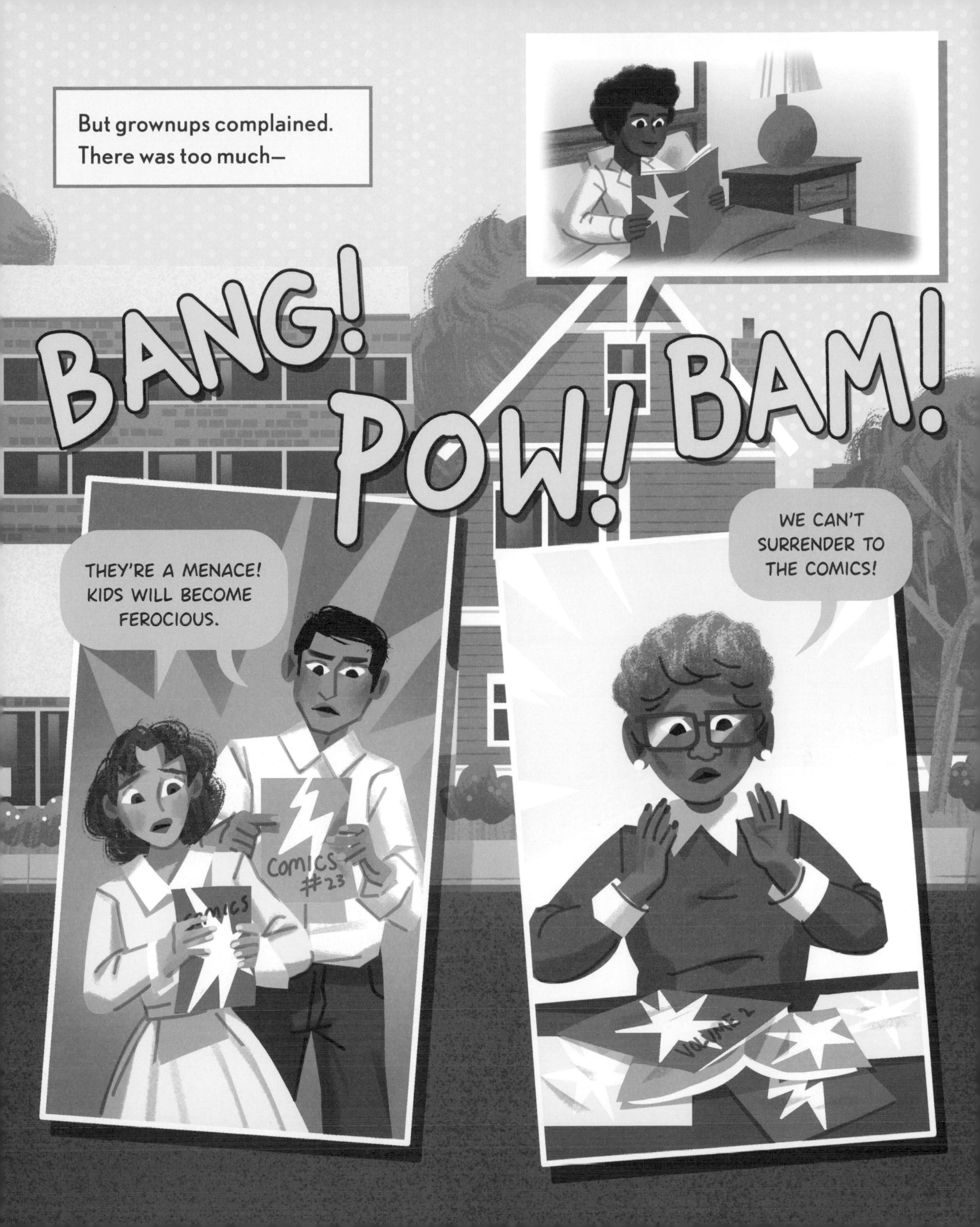

But grownups complained.
There was too much—
BANG!
POW!
BAM!
THEY'RE A MENACE! KIDS WILL BECOME FEROCIOUS.
COMICS #23
COMICS
WE CAN'T SURRENDER TO THE COMICS!
VOLUME 2

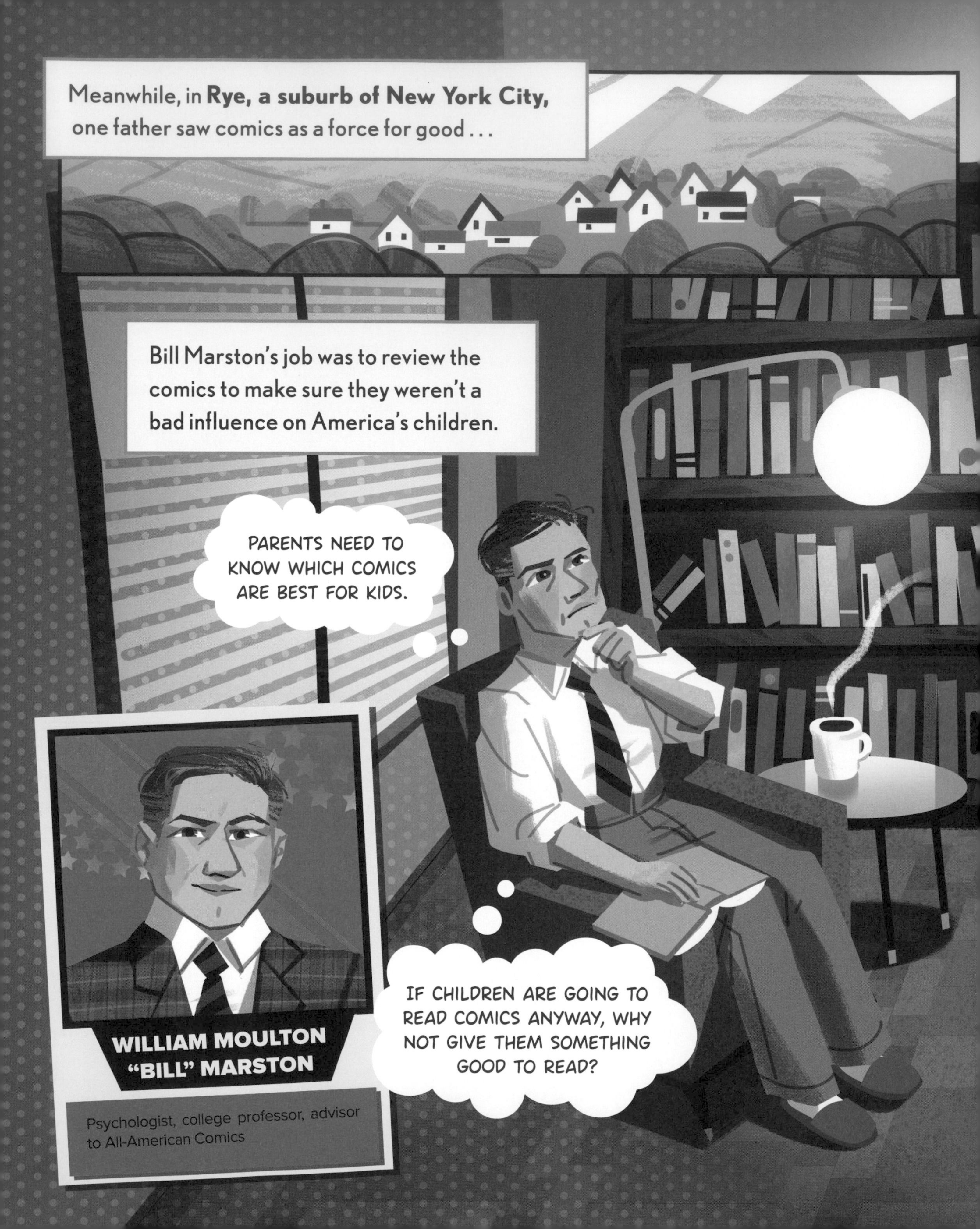
Meanwhile, in **Rye, a suburb of New York City,** one father saw comics as a force for good . . .
Bill Marston's job was to review the comics to make sure they weren't a bad influence on America's children.
PARENTS NEED TO KNOW WHICH COMICS ARE BEST FOR KIDS.
WILLIAM MOULTON "BILL" MARSTON
Psychologist, college professor, advisor to All-American Comics
IF CHILDREN ARE GOING TO READ COMICS ANYWAY, WHY NOT GIVE THEM SOMETHING GOOD TO READ?

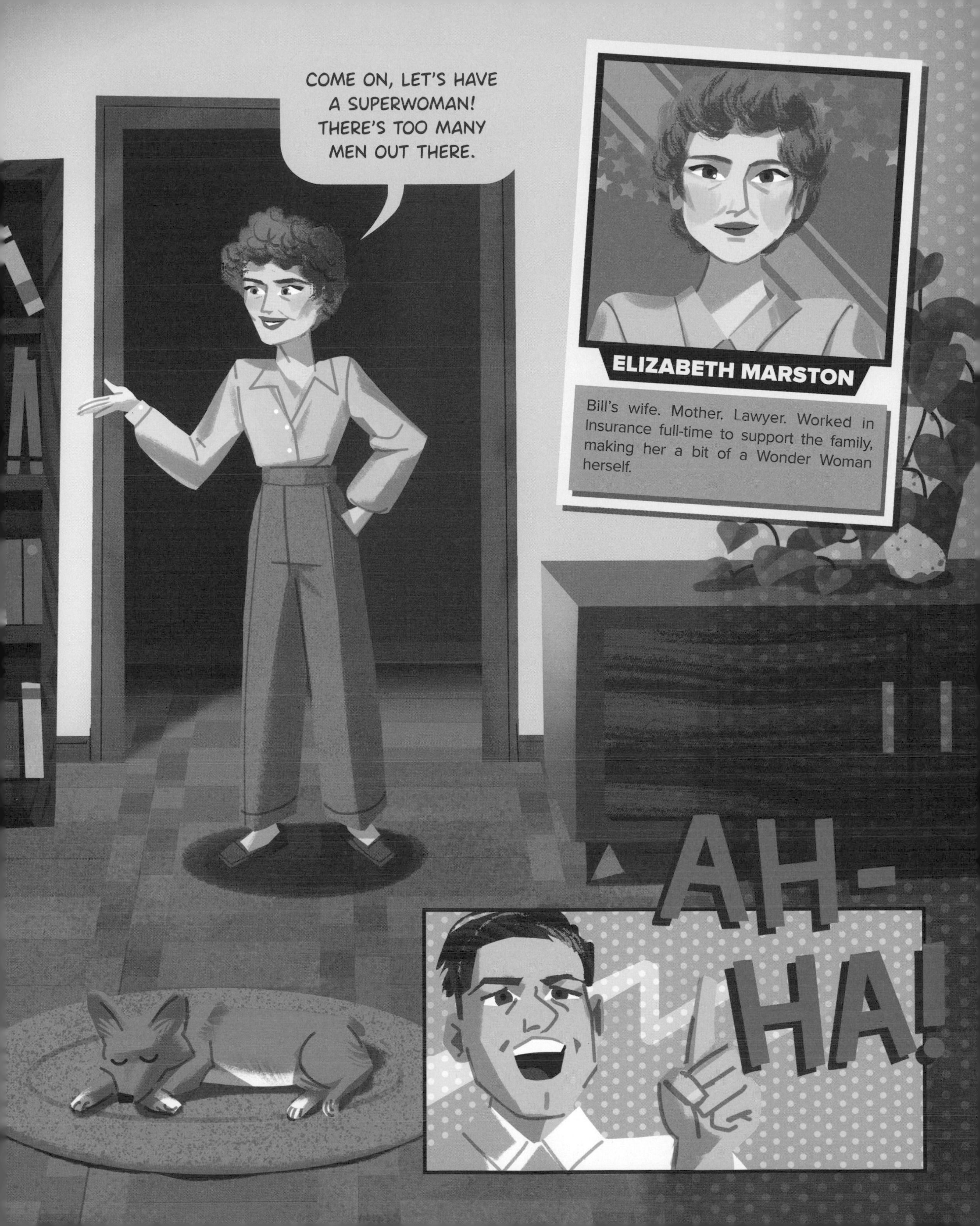
COME ON, LET'S HAVE A SUPERWOMAN! THERE'S TOO MANY MEN OUT THERE.
ELIZABETH MARSTON
Bill's wife. Mother. Lawyer. Worked in Insurance full-time to support the family, making her a bit of a Wonder Woman herself.
AH-HA!

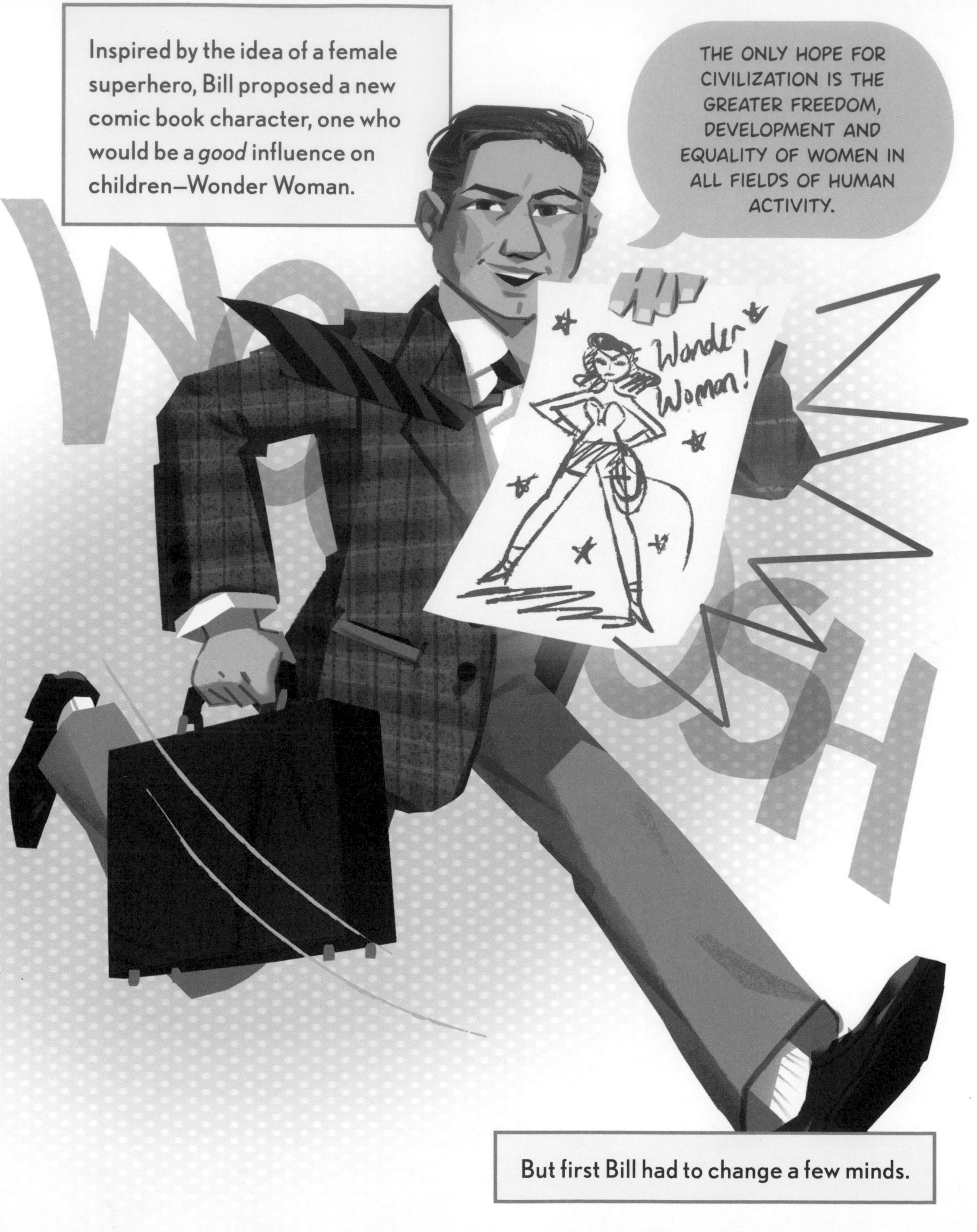
Inspired by the idea of a female superhero, Bill proposed a new comic book character, one who would be a *good* influence on children—Wonder Woman.
THE ONLY HOPE FOR CIVILIZATION IS THE GREATER FREEDOM, DEVELOPMENT AND EQUALITY OF WOMEN IN ALL FIELDS OF HUMAN ACTIVITY.
Wonder Woman!
But first Bill had to change a few minds.

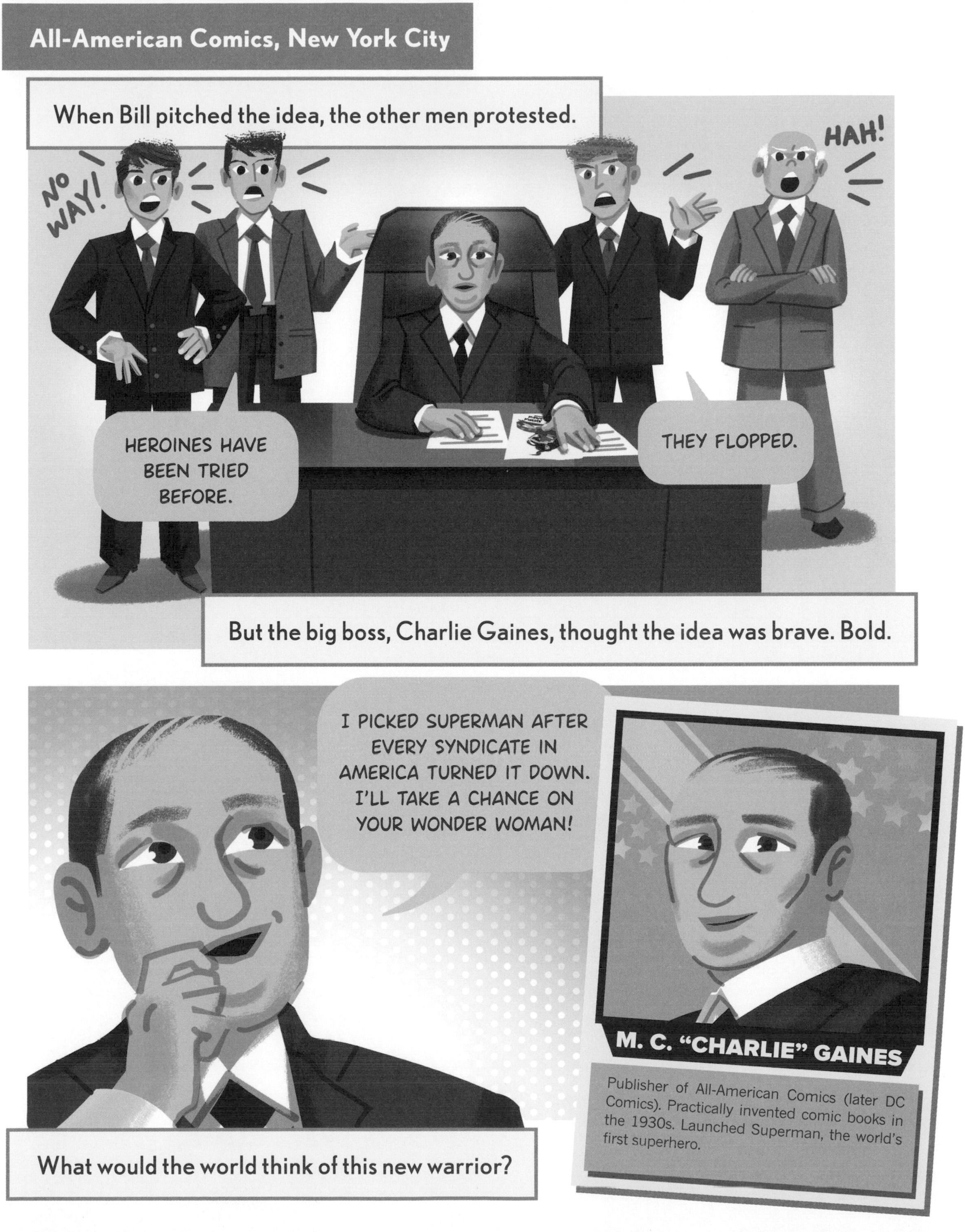
All-American Comics, New York City
When Bill pitched the idea, the other men protested.
NO WAY!
HAH!
HEROINES HAVE BEEN TRIED BEFORE.
THEY FLOPPED.
But the big boss, Charlie Gaines, thought the idea was brave. Bold.
I PICKED SUPERMAN AFTER EVERY SYNDICATE IN AMERICA TURNED IT DOWN. I'LL TAKE A CHANCE ON YOUR WONDER WOMAN!
What would the world think of this new warrior?
M. C. "CHARLIE" GAINES
Publisher of All-American Comics (later DC Comics). Practically invented comic books in the 1930s. Launched Superman, the world's first superhero.

Across America . . .
NO
NO WW
Parents protested.
NO WONDER WOMAN!
LOOK AT HER COSTUME. IT'S OUTRAGEOUS!
But kids loved her. Her comics flew off the racks, sometimes outselling the supermen.

And when the Justice Society, the first-ever superhero team, needed a new member, kids sent in their votes by the hundreds.

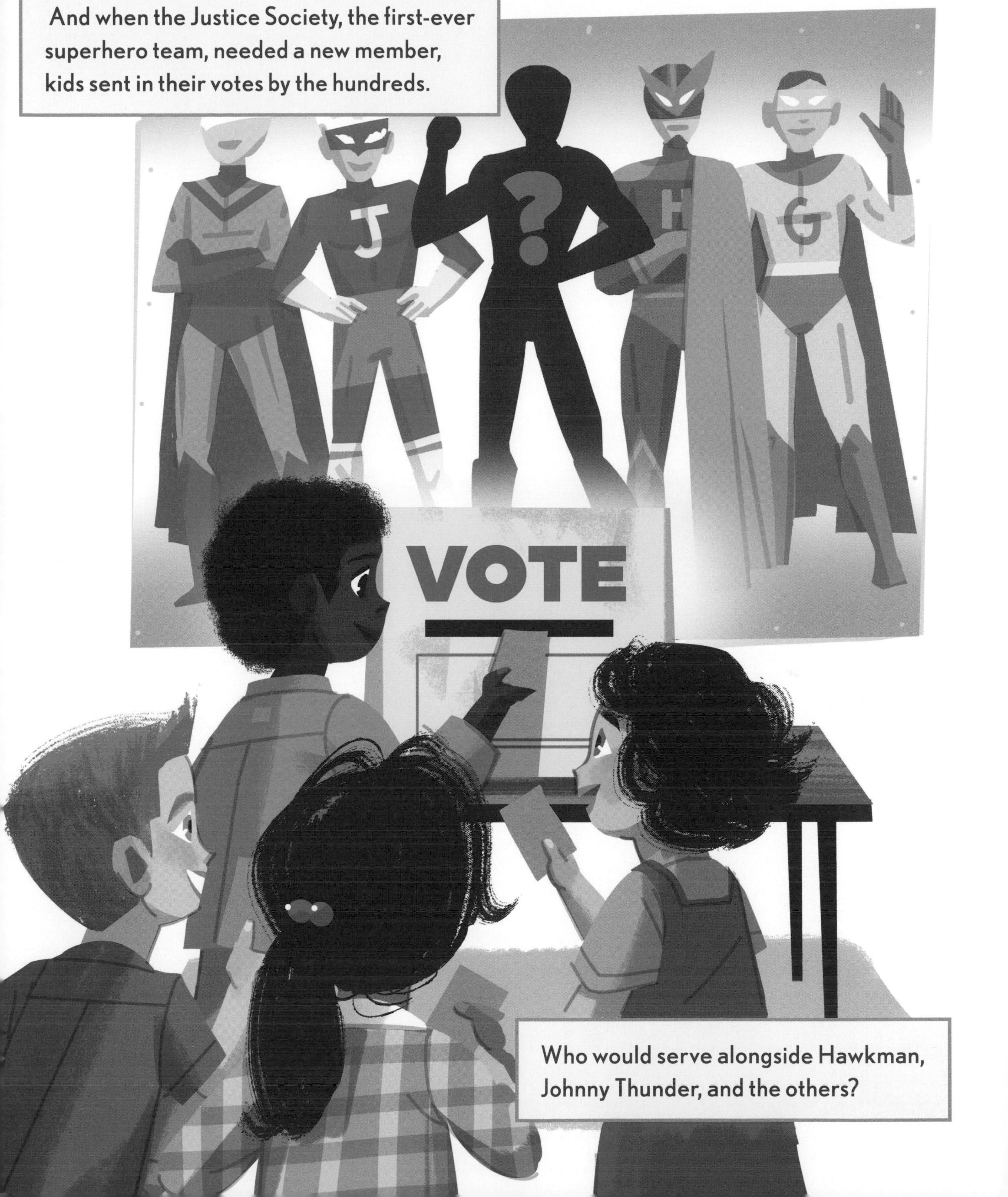
VOTE

Who would serve alongside Hawkman, Johnny Thunder, and the others?

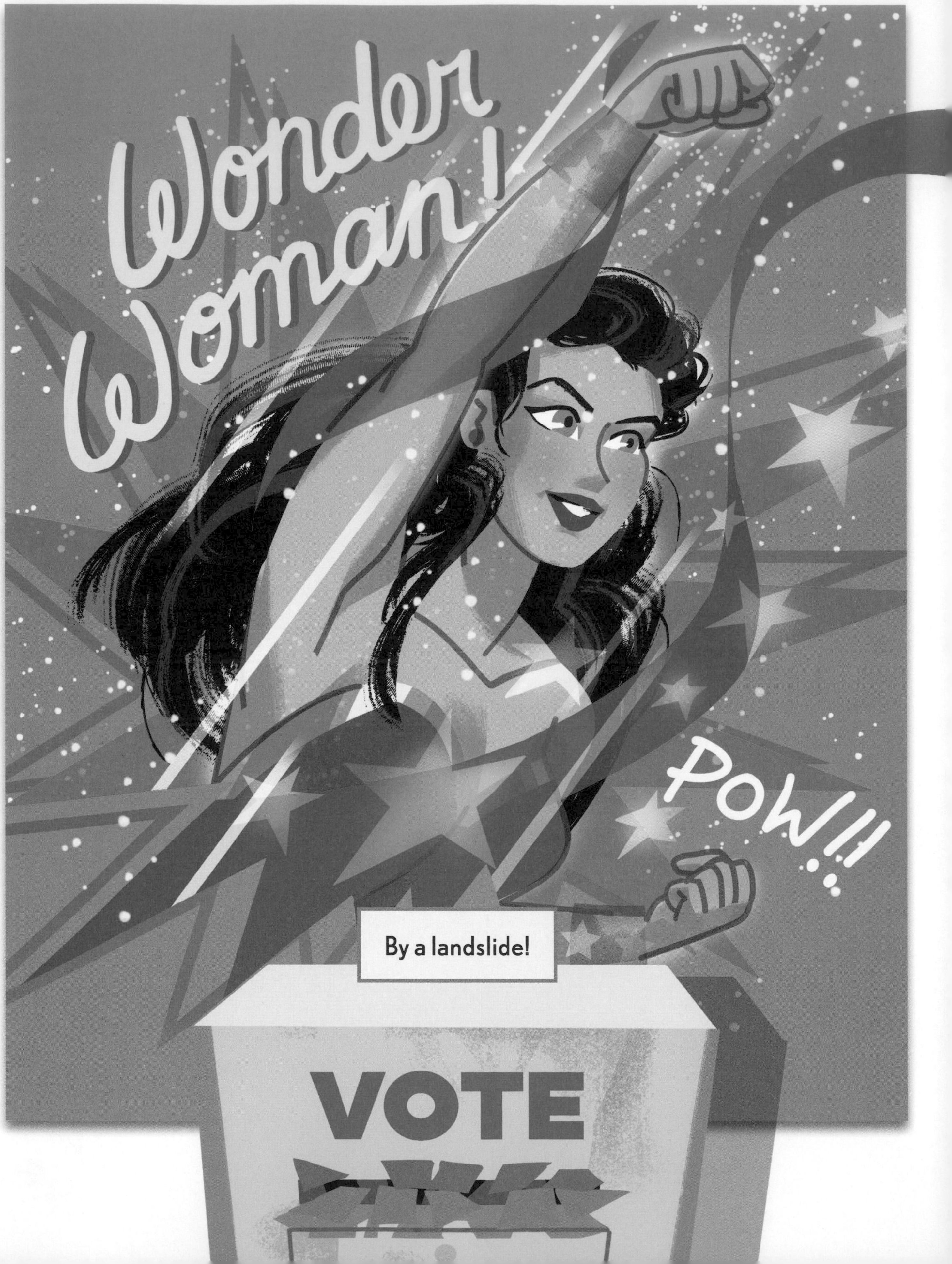
Wonder Woman!
POW!!
By a landslide!
VOTE

In issue after issue, she showed kids what women could do:

Serve as a nurse (as Diana Prince) . . .

. . . and capture enemy soldiers (as Wonder Woman) in World War II.

SWISH!
FAIR PAY!
EQUAL PAY!
RIGHTS
= PAY
YEAH!
VOTE!

Crusade for equal pay.

Become president of the United States!

Plus *Wonder Woman* comics were about to get a new feature, showcasing inspiring true stories of real women and how they'd changed the world.

1942. Retired tennis pro Alice Marble and Charlie Gaines discuss the comic book craze.

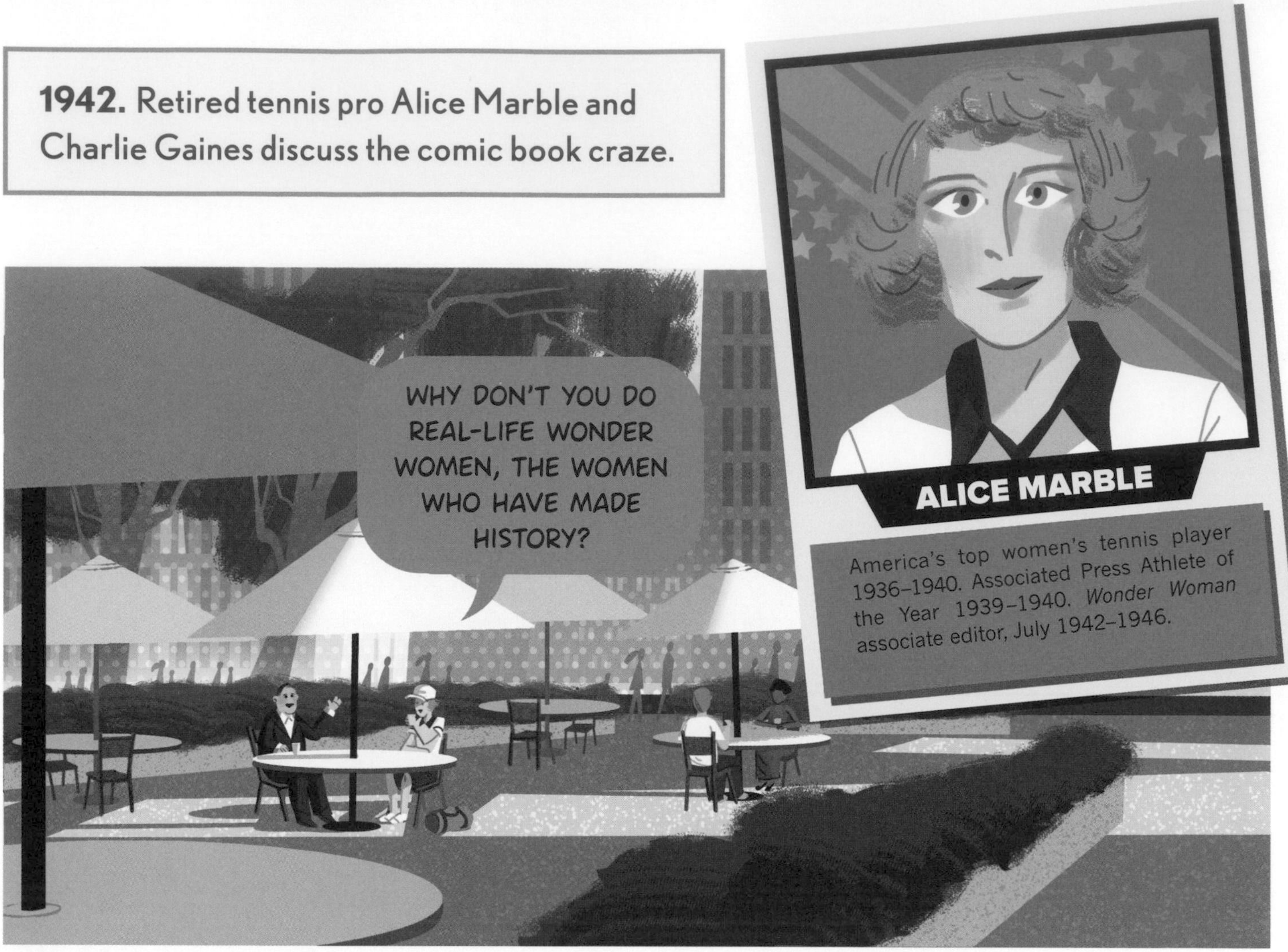

ALICE MARBLE
America's top women's tennis player 1936–1940. Associated Press Athlete of the Year 1939–1940. *Wonder Woman* associate editor, July 1942–1946.
WHY DON'T YOU DO REAL-LIFE WONDER WOMEN, THE WOMEN WHO HAVE MADE HISTORY?

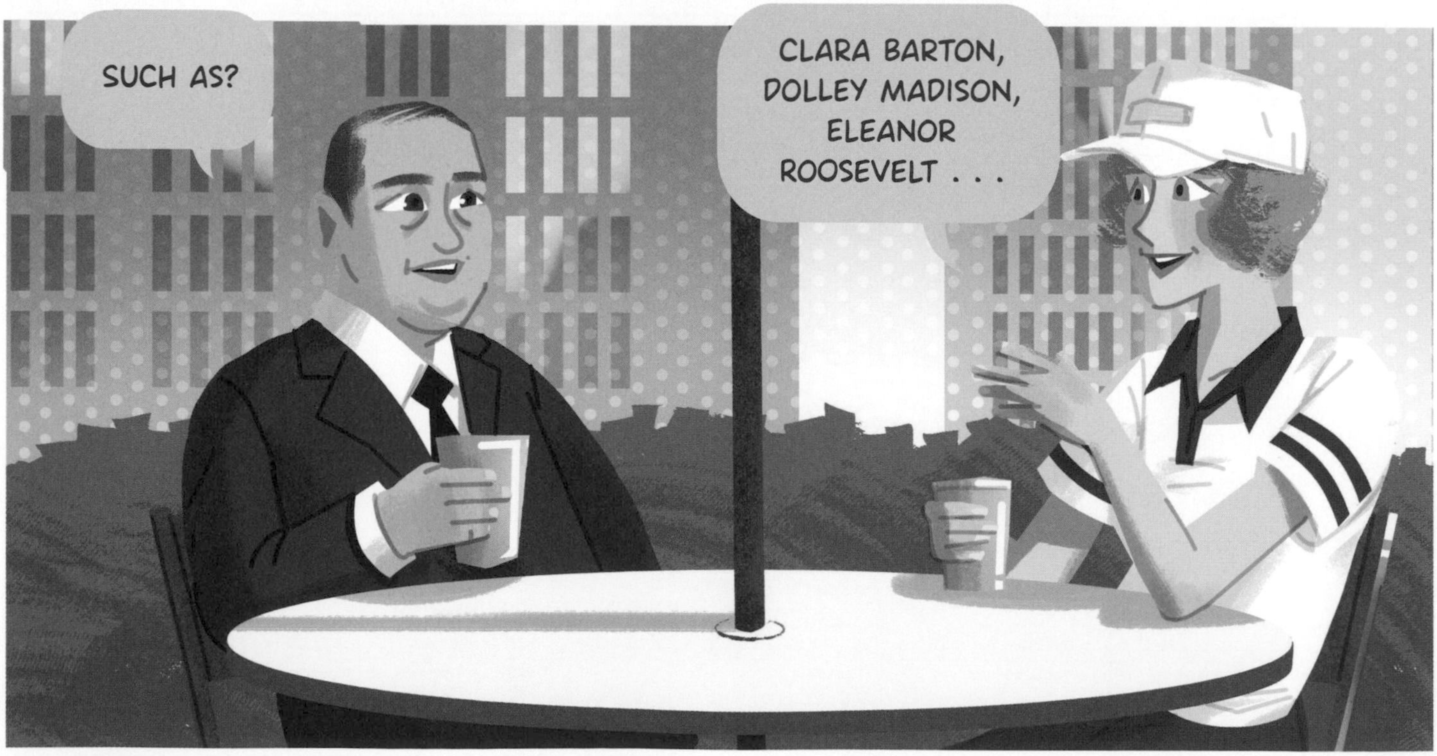

SUCH AS?
CLARA BARTON, DOLLEY MADISON, ELEANOR ROOSEVELT . . .

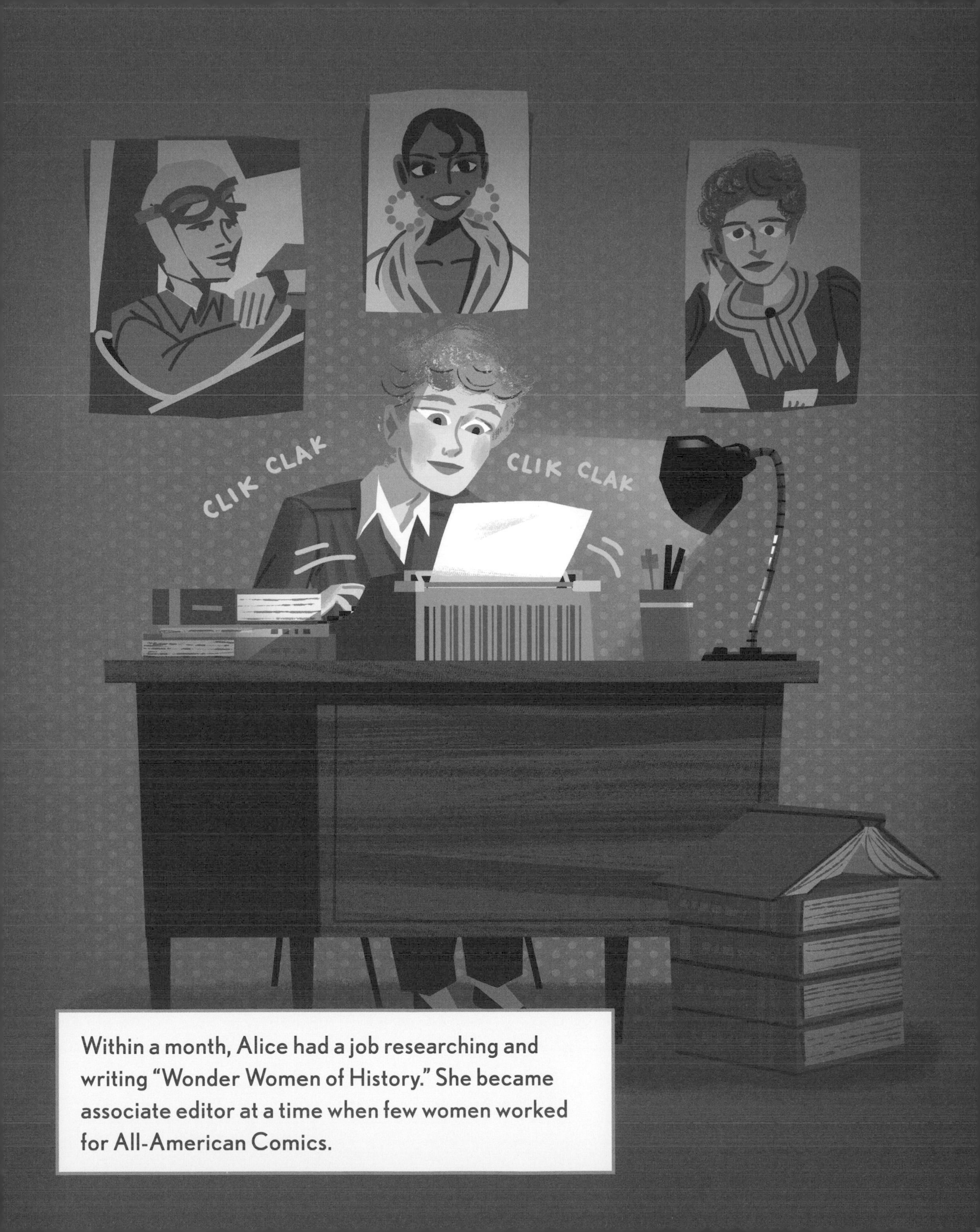
CLIK CLAK
CLIK CLAK

Within a month, Alice had a job researching and writing "Wonder Women of History." She became associate editor at a time when few women worked for All-American Comics.

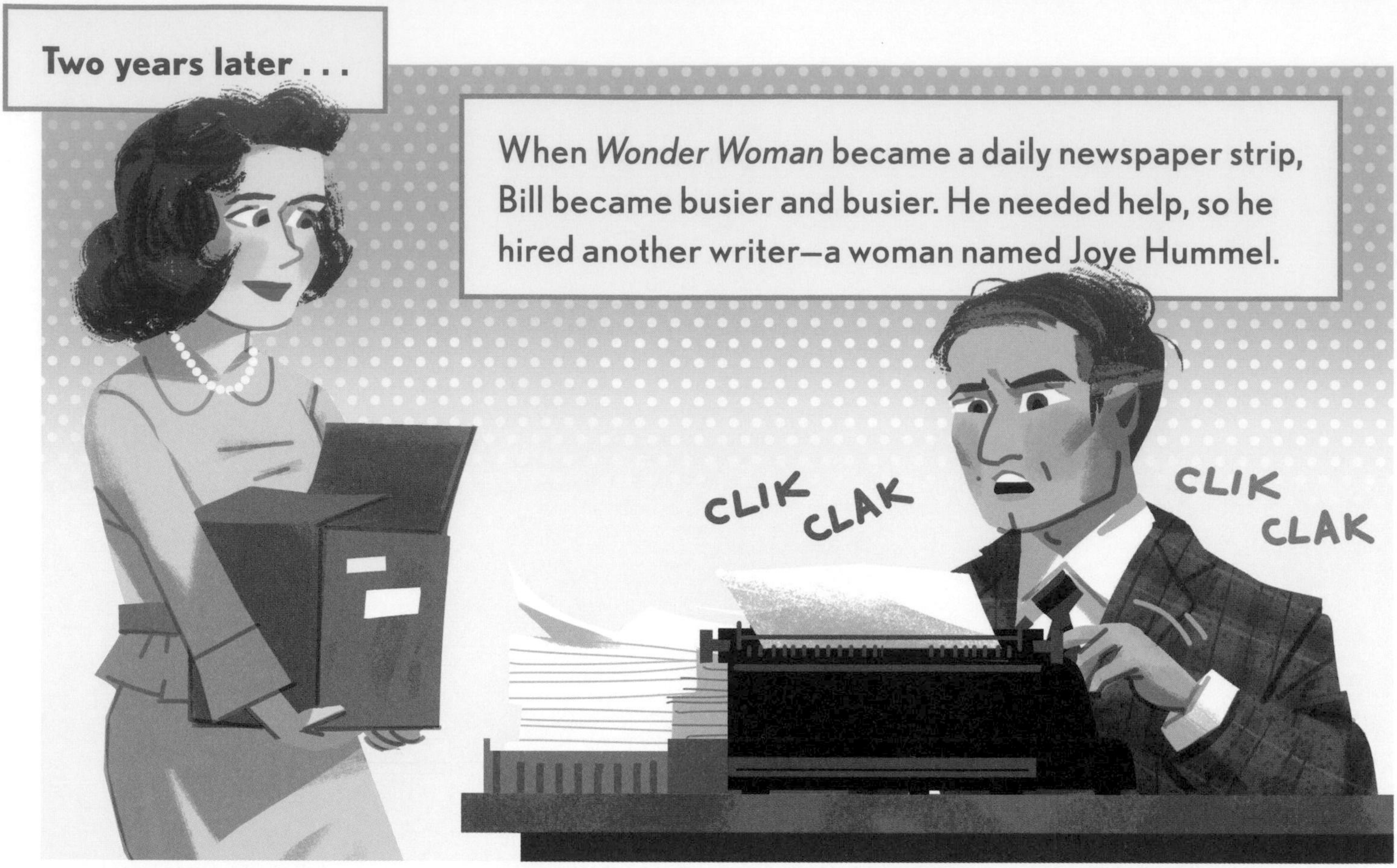
Two years later . . .
When *Wonder Woman* became a daily newspaper strip, Bill became busier and busier. He needed help, so he hired another writer—a woman named Joye Hummel.
CLIK CLAK
CLIK CLAK

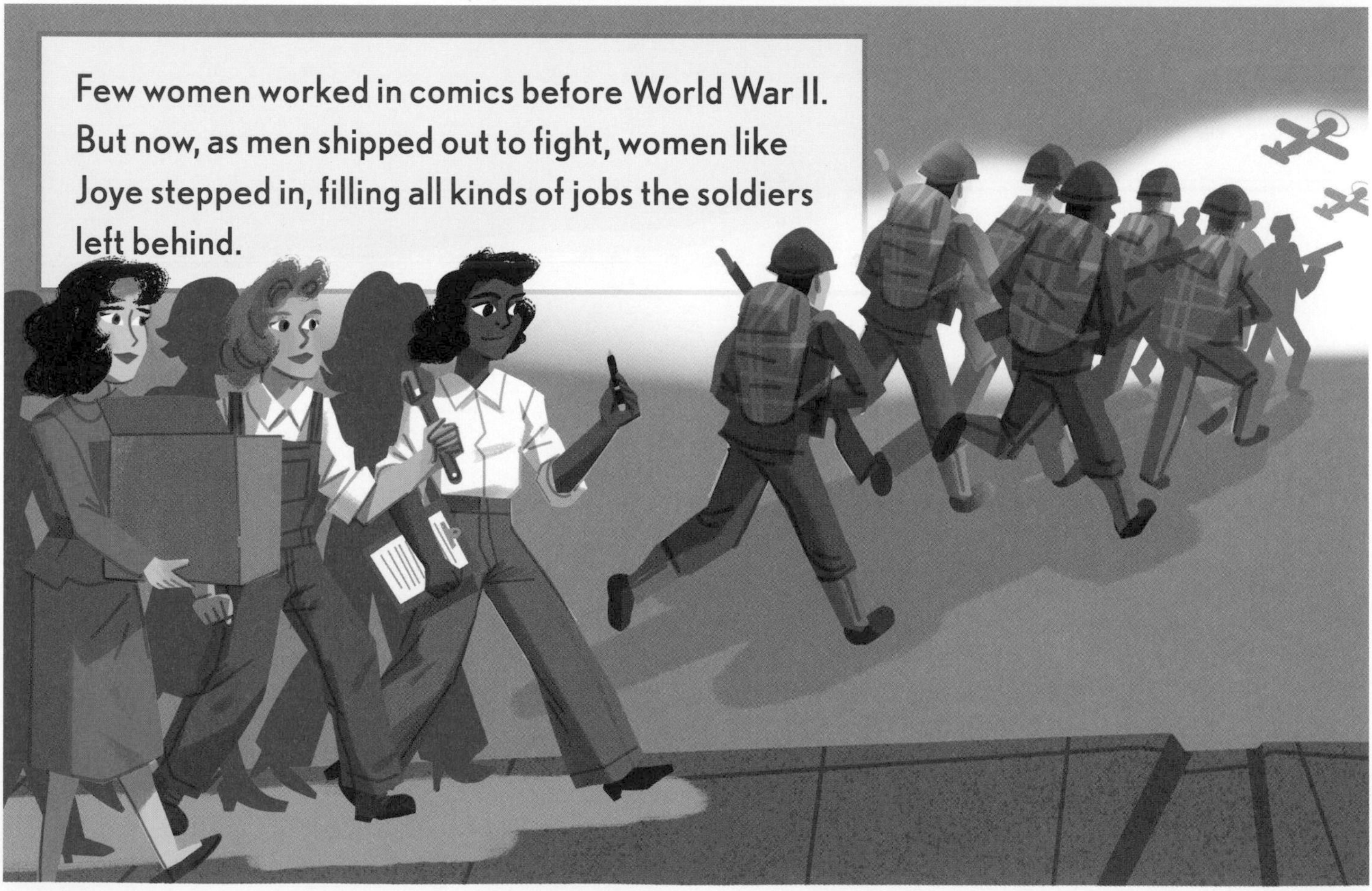
Few women worked in comics before World War II. But now, as men shipped out to fight, women like Joye stepped in, filling all kinds of jobs the soldiers left behind.

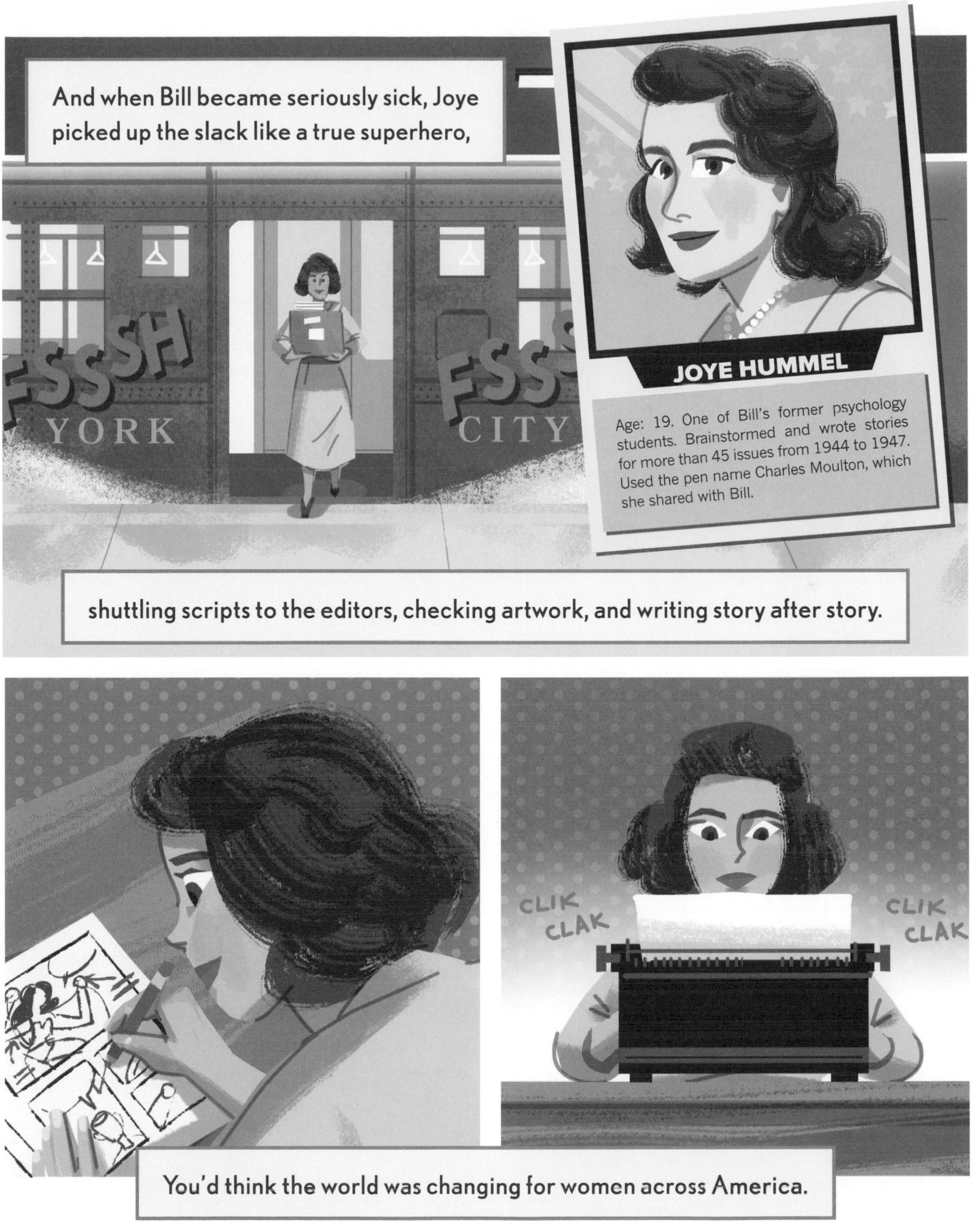
And when Bill became seriously sick, Joye picked up the slack like a true superhero,
FSSSH
YORK
FSSS
CITY
JOYE HUMMEL
Age: 19. One of Bill's former psychology students. Brainstormed and wrote stories for more than 45 issues from 1944 to 1947. Used the pen name Charles Moulton, which she shared with Bill.
shuttling scripts to the editors, checking artwork, and writing story after story.
CLIK CLAK
CLIK CLAK
You'd think the world was changing for women across America.

But then World War II ended, and people were weary of fighting.

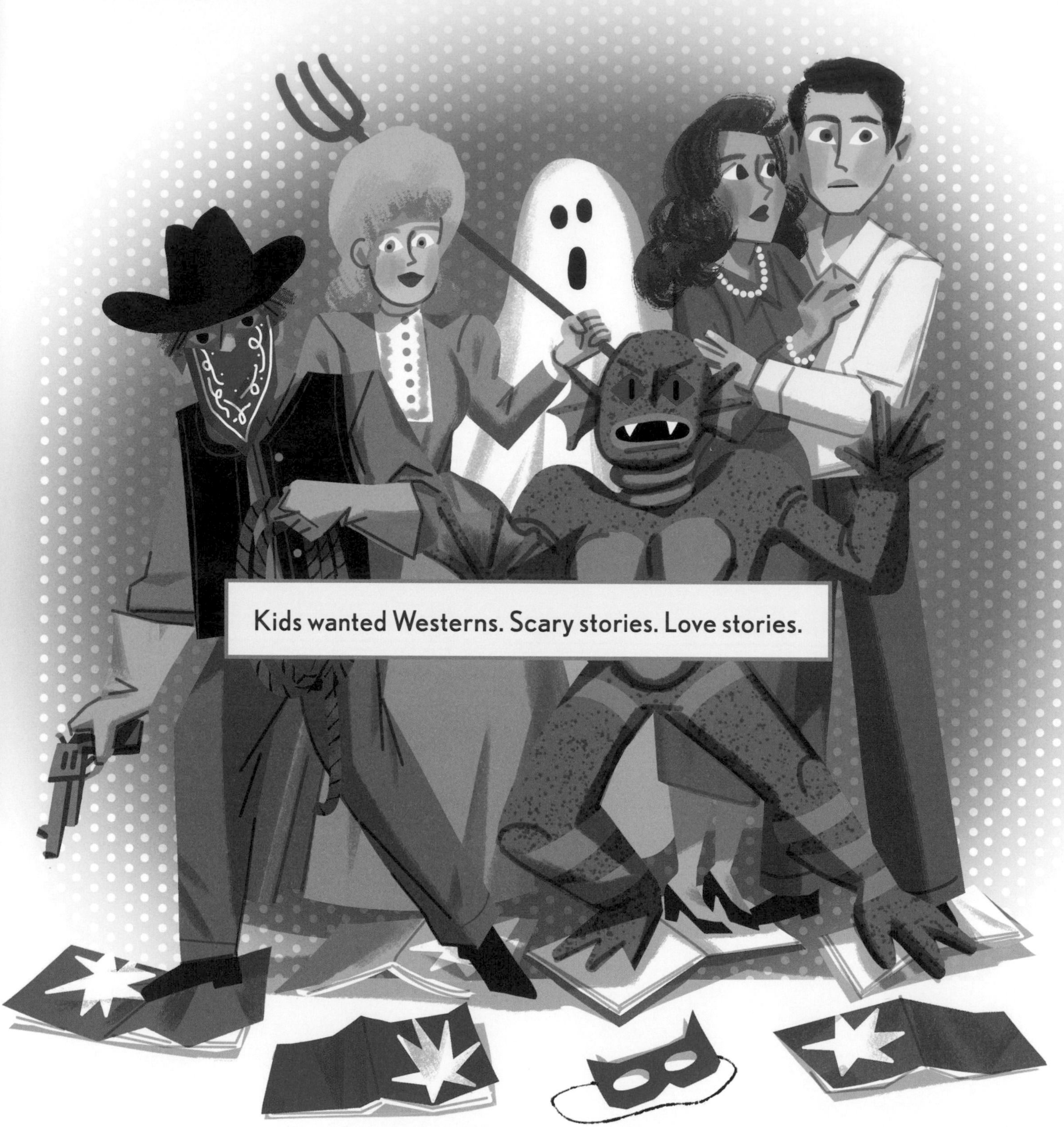

Kids wanted Westerns. Scary stories. Love stories.

Sales slumped as patriotic superheroes fell out of favor.

In real life, women who'd turned rivets and cracked codes during World War II found themselves out of work and back at home.

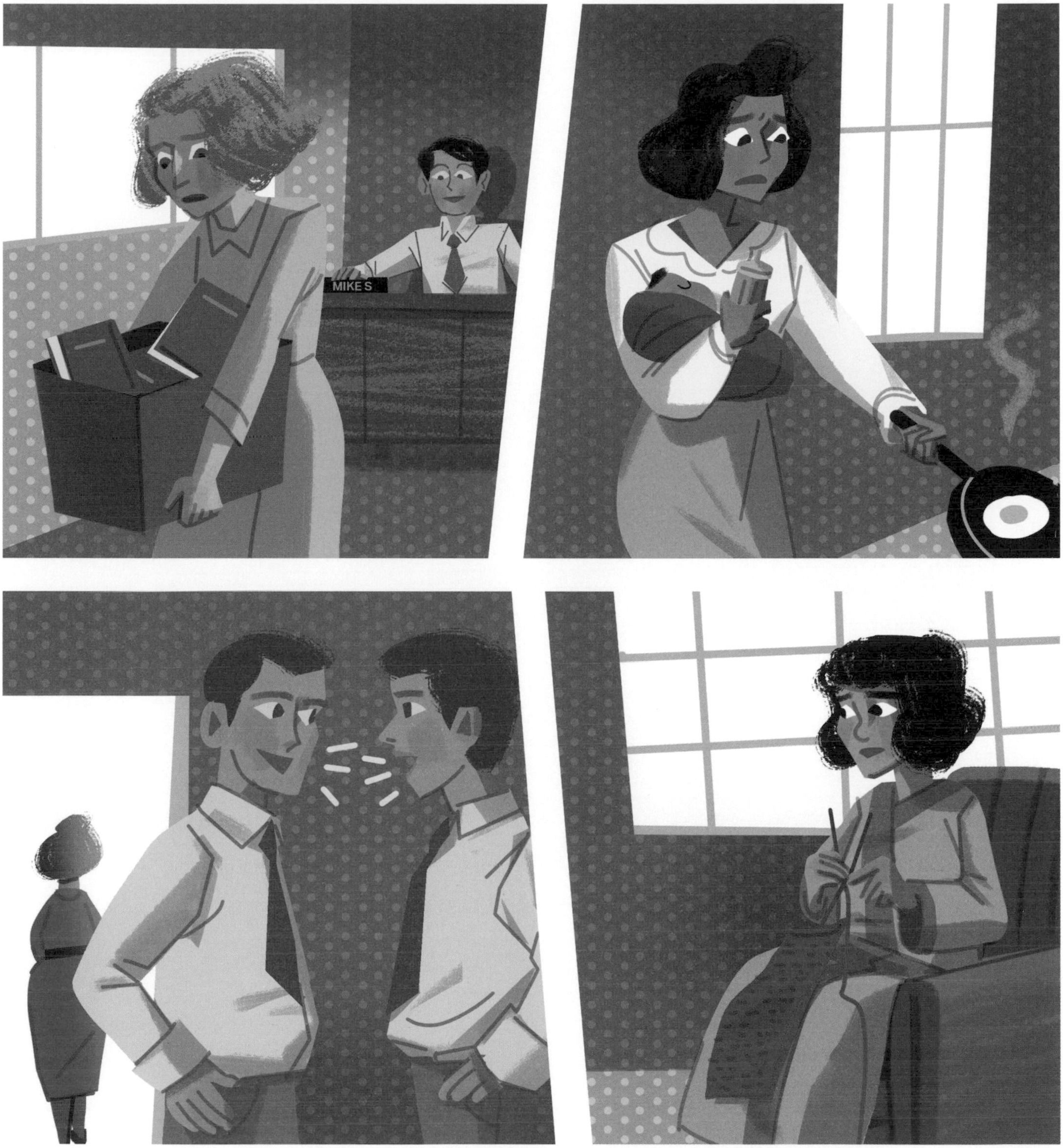
MIKE S

Men needed their jobs back. Women were told to refocus on home and family.

And so did Wonder Woman.

She now had a new creative team. Bill had died. Joye had left her job to become a wife and mother. The new crew didn't care about painting the Amazon princess as a strong and powerful role model.

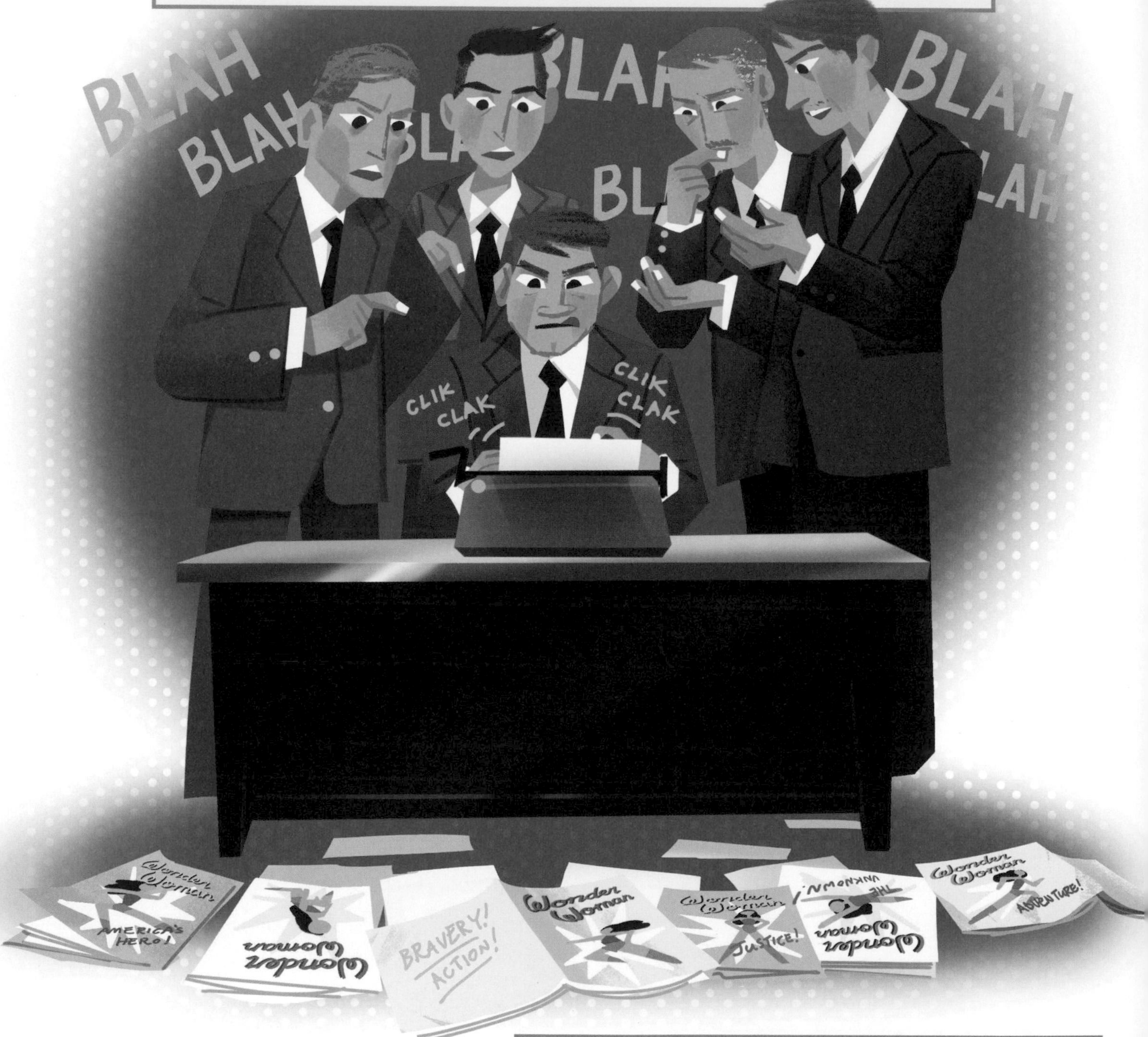
BLAH
BLAH
BLAH
BLAH
CLIK
CLAK
CLIK
CLAK
Wonder Woman
AMERICA'S HERO!
Wonder Woman
BRAVERY!
ACTION!
Wonder Woman
Wonder Woman
JUSTICE!
THE UNKNOWN!
Wonder Woman
Wonder Woman
ADVENTURE!

Despite what *Wonder Woman* promised, the world hadn't changed much for women at all.

1950s America

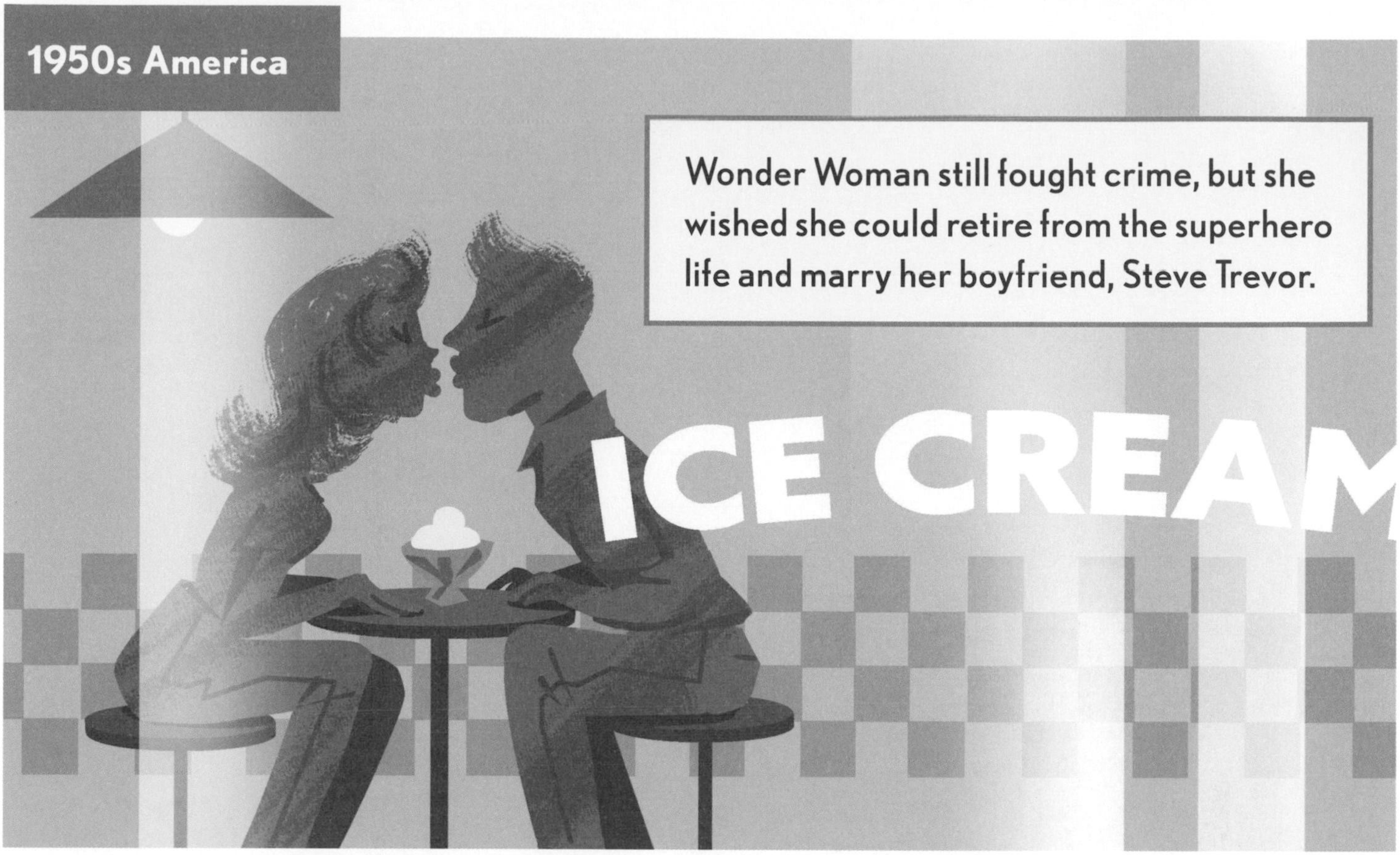
ICE CREAM

Wonder Woman still fought crime, but she wished she could retire from the superhero life and marry her boyfriend, Steve Trevor.

Instead of "Wonder Women of History," her comics got new features in the 1950s, focused on fashion, beauty, and marriage customs around the world!

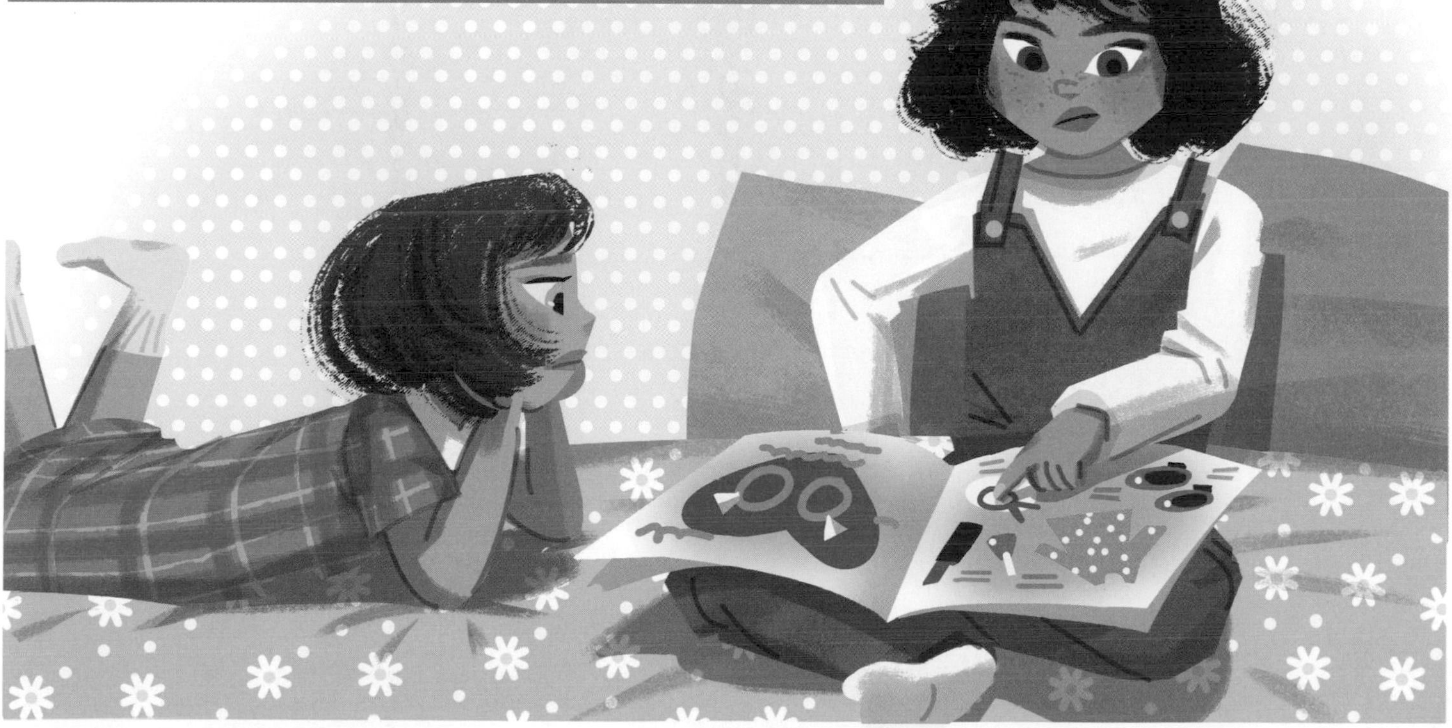

Then the **1960s** arrived.

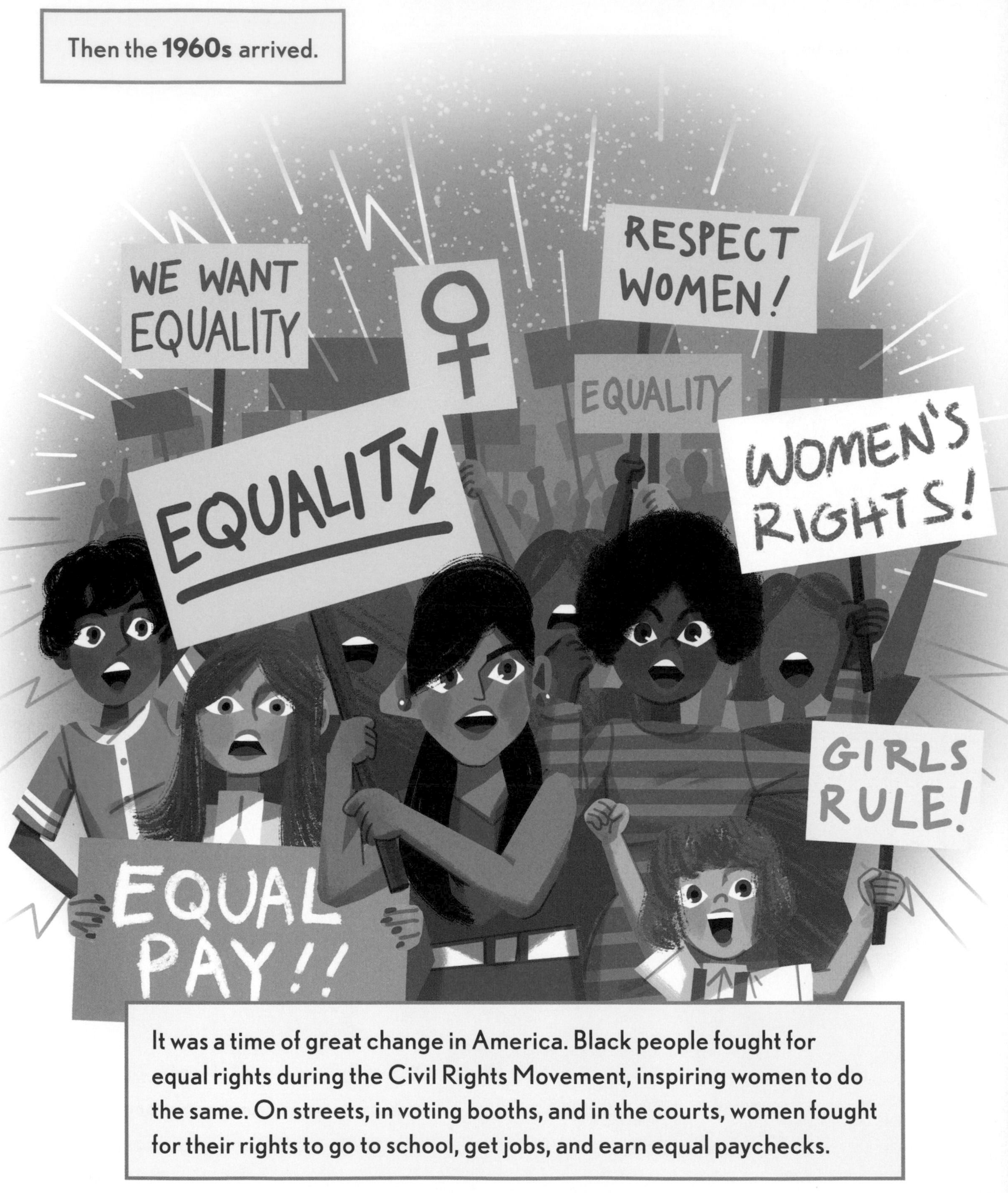
WE WANT EQUALITY
RESPECT WOMEN!
♀
EQUALITY
EQUALITY
WOMEN'S RIGHTS!
GIRLS RULE!
EQUAL PAY!!

It was a time of great change in America. Black people fought for equal rights during the Civil Rights Movement, inspiring women to do the same. On streets, in voting booths, and in the courts, women fought for their rights to go to school, get jobs, and earn equal paychecks.

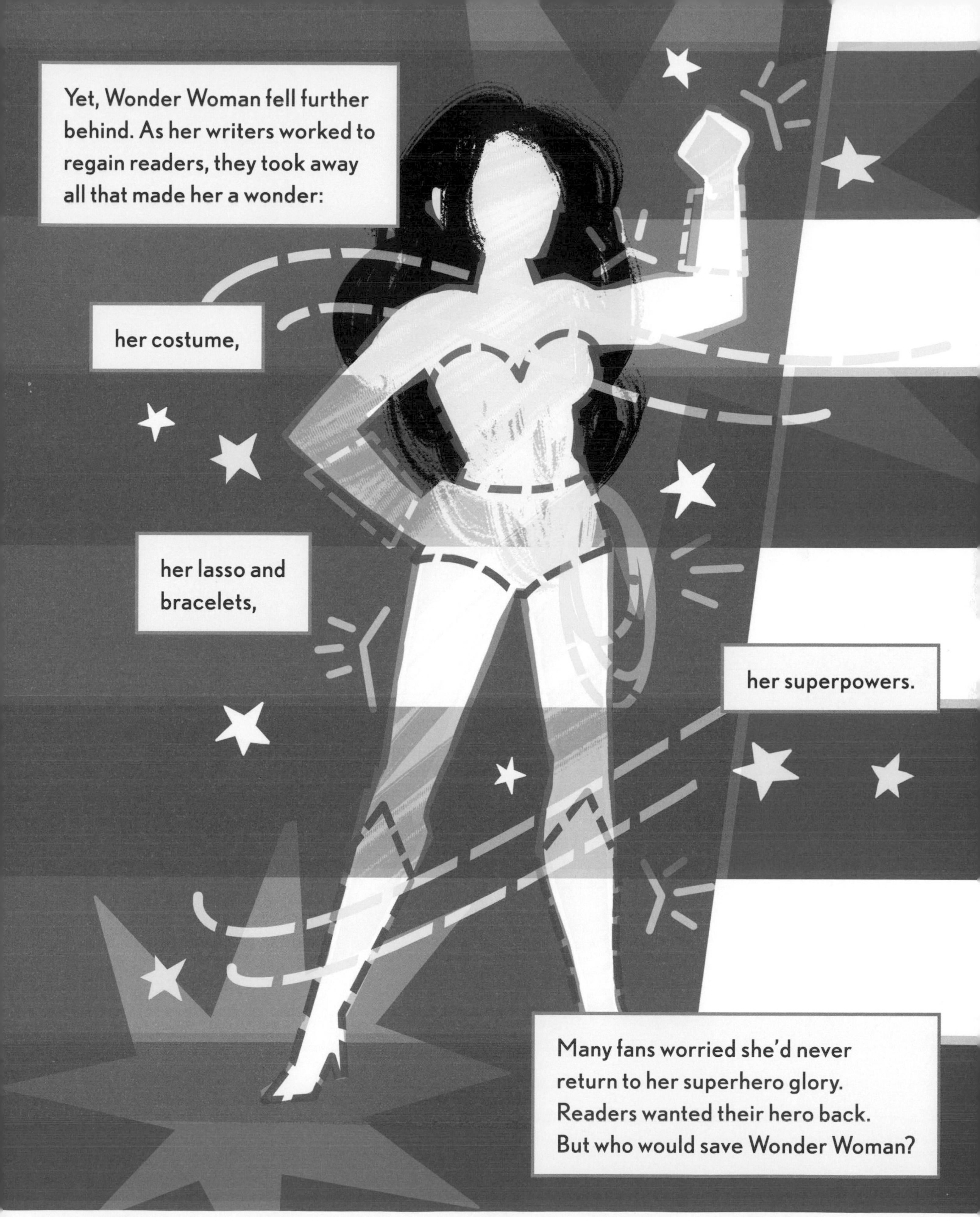
Yet, Wonder Woman fell further behind. As her writers worked to regain readers, they took away all that made her a wonder:
her costume,
her lasso and bracelets,
her superpowers.
Many fans worried she'd never return to her superhero glory. Readers wanted their hero back. But who would save Wonder Woman?

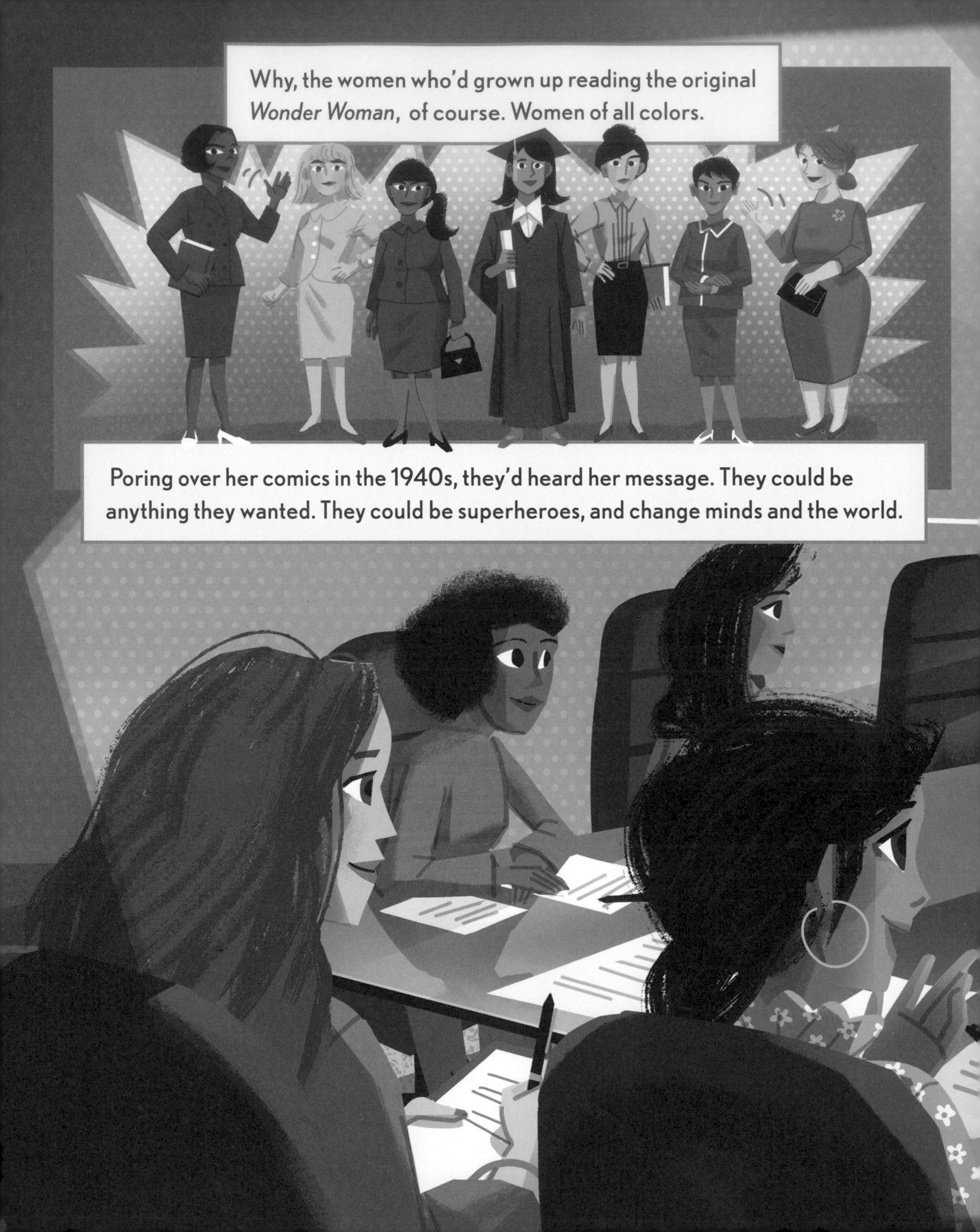
Why, the women who'd grown up reading the original *Wonder Woman*, of course. Women of all colors.
Poring over her comics in the 1940s, they'd heard her message. They could be anything they wanted. They could be superheroes, and change minds and the world.

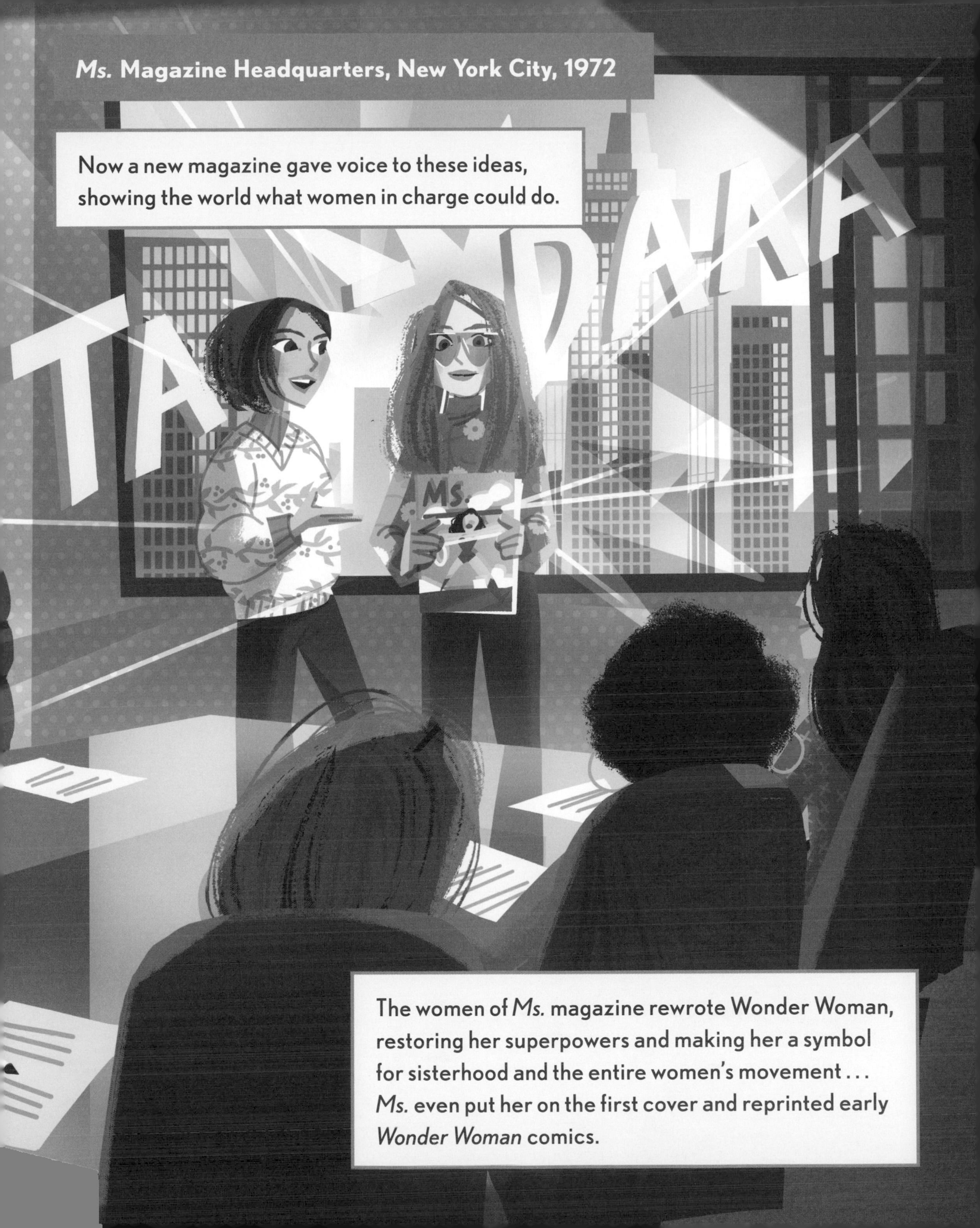
Ms. Magazine Headquarters, New York City, 1972
Now a new magazine gave voice to these ideas, showing the world what women in charge could do.
TA DAAA
Ms.
The women of *Ms.* magazine rewrote Wonder Woman, restoring her superpowers and making her a symbol for sisterhood and the entire women's movement . . . *Ms.* even put her on the first cover and reprinted early *Wonder Woman* comics.

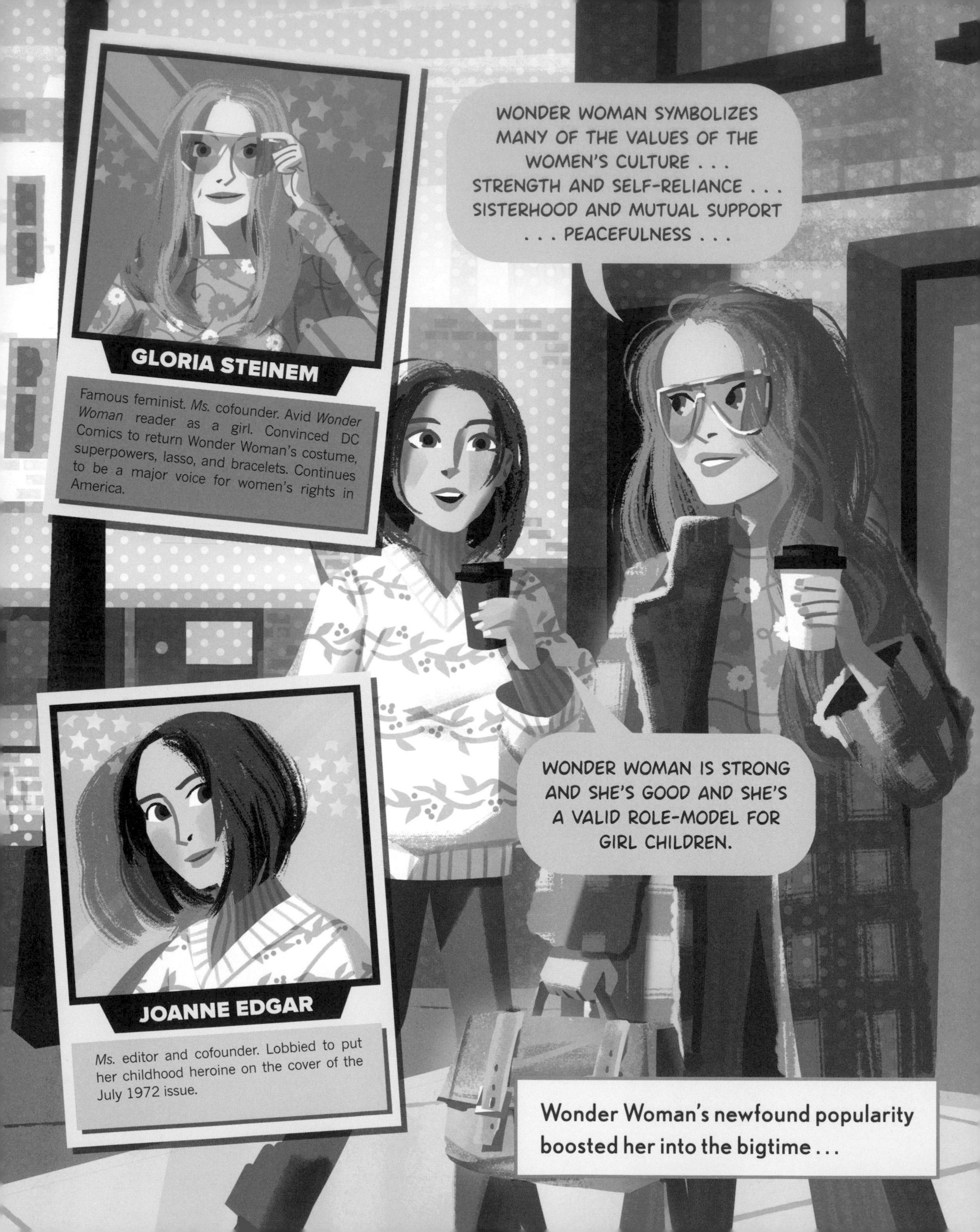
GLORIA STEINEM
Famous feminist. Ms. cofounder. Avid Wonder Woman reader as a girl. Convinced DC Comics to return Wonder Woman's costume, superpowers, lasso, and bracelets. Continues to be a major voice for women's rights in America.
WONDER WOMAN SYMBOLIZES MANY OF THE VALUES OF THE WOMEN'S CULTURE . . . STRENGTH AND SELF-RELIANCE . . . SISTERHOOD AND MUTUAL SUPPORT . . . PEACEFULNESS . . .
JOANNE EDGAR
Ms. editor and cofounder. Lobbied to put her childhood heroine on the cover of the July 1972 issue.
WONDER WOMAN IS STRONG AND SHE'S GOOD AND SHE'S A VALID ROLE-MODEL FOR GIRL CHILDREN.
Wonder Woman's newfound popularity boosted her into the bigtime . . .

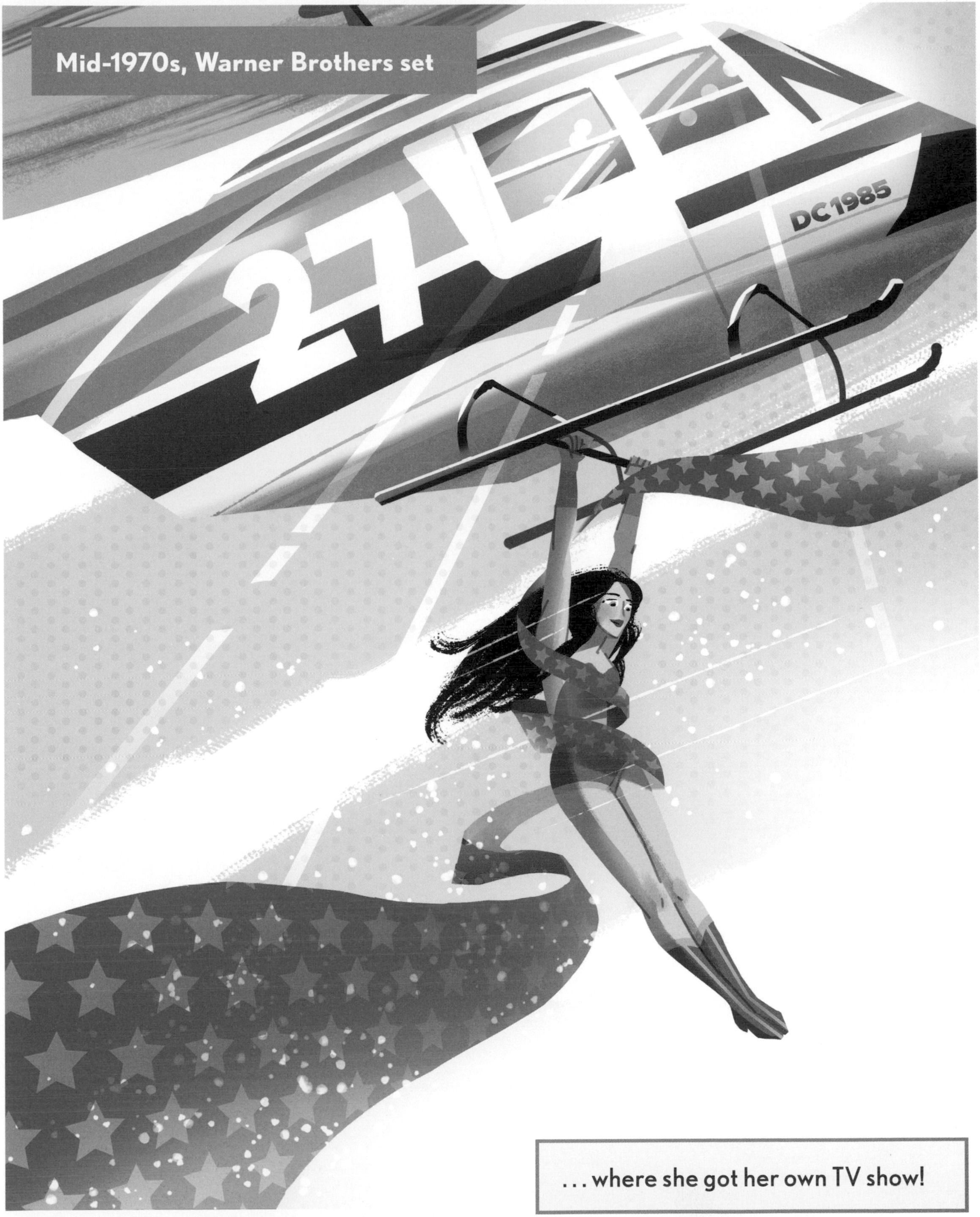
Mid-1970s, Warner Brothers set
DC1985
. . . where she got her own TV show!

As Wonder Woman, actress Lynda Carter fought bad guys and stood up for other women. At first, TV networks weren't sure people would tune in to watch a female superhero. But Lynda won them over, getting piles of fan mail for her performance.

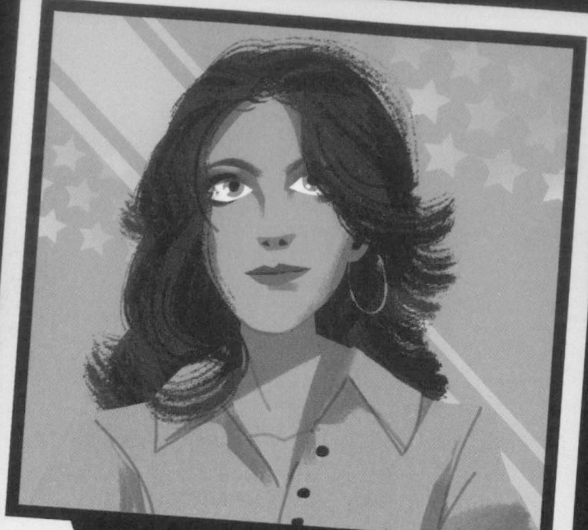

LYNDA CARTER

Actress. Singer. Totally unknown when cast as Wonder Woman. Became one of the first women to lead an hour-long, action-packed TV show. Performed some of her own stunts at a time when few women did stunts at all.

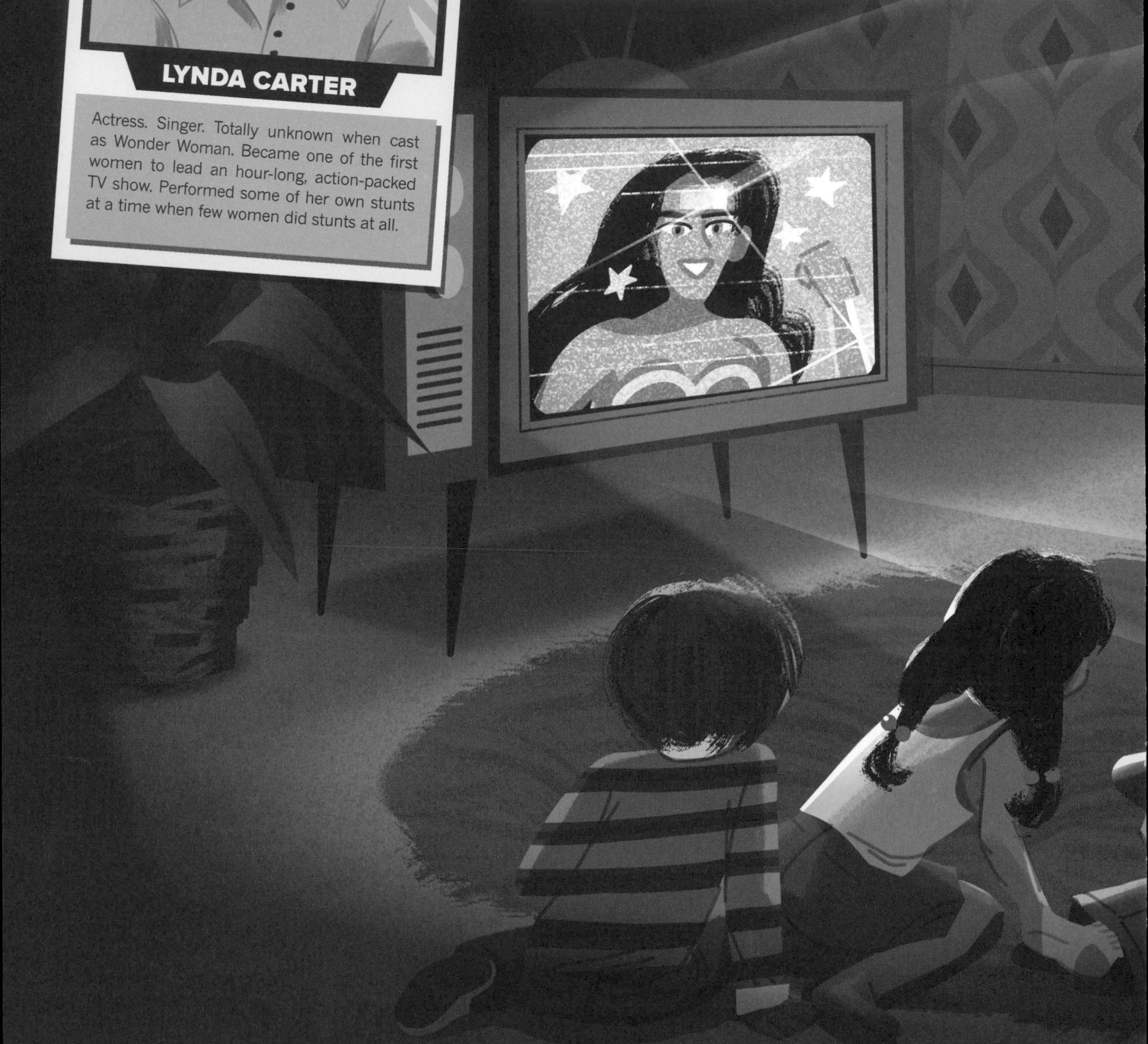

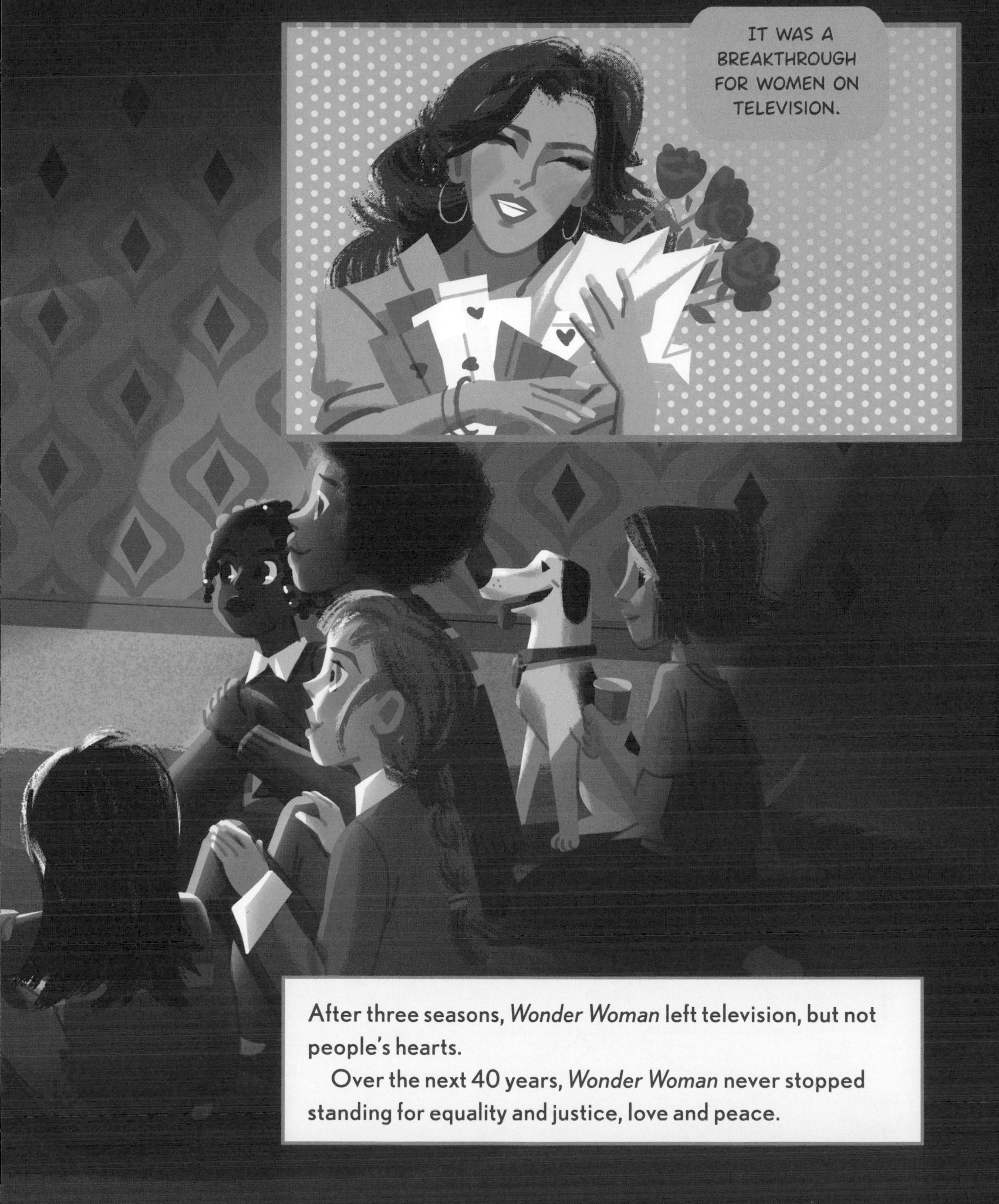
IT WAS A BREAKTHROUGH FOR WOMEN ON TELEVISION.

After three seasons, *Wonder Woman* left television, but not people's hearts.

Over the next 40 years, *Wonder Woman* never stopped standing for equality and justice, love and peace.

Present day

And a new world began to take shape . . .

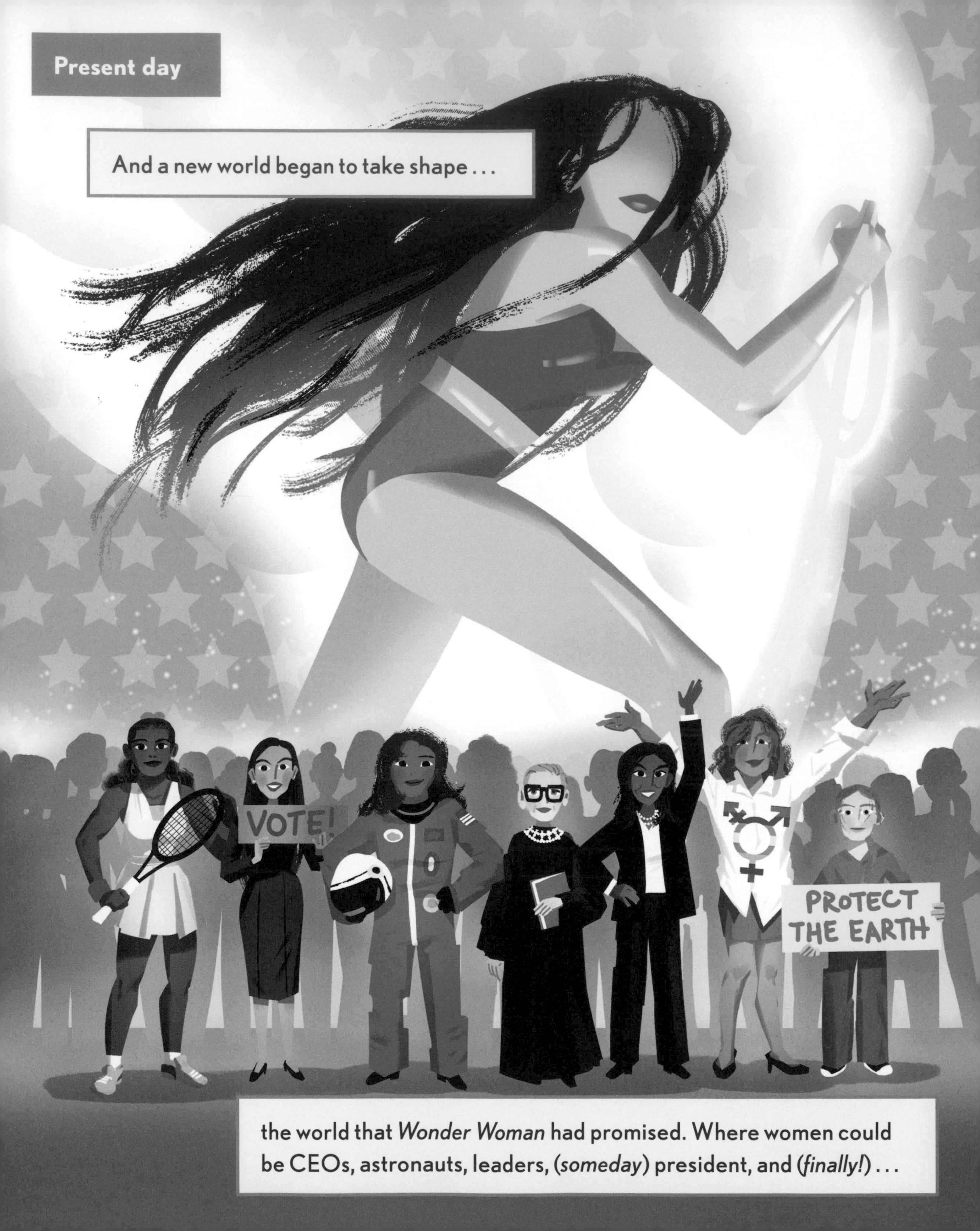
VOTE!
PROTECT THE EARTH

the world that *Wonder Woman* had promised. Where women could be CEOs, astronauts, leaders, (*someday*) president, and (*finally!*) . . .

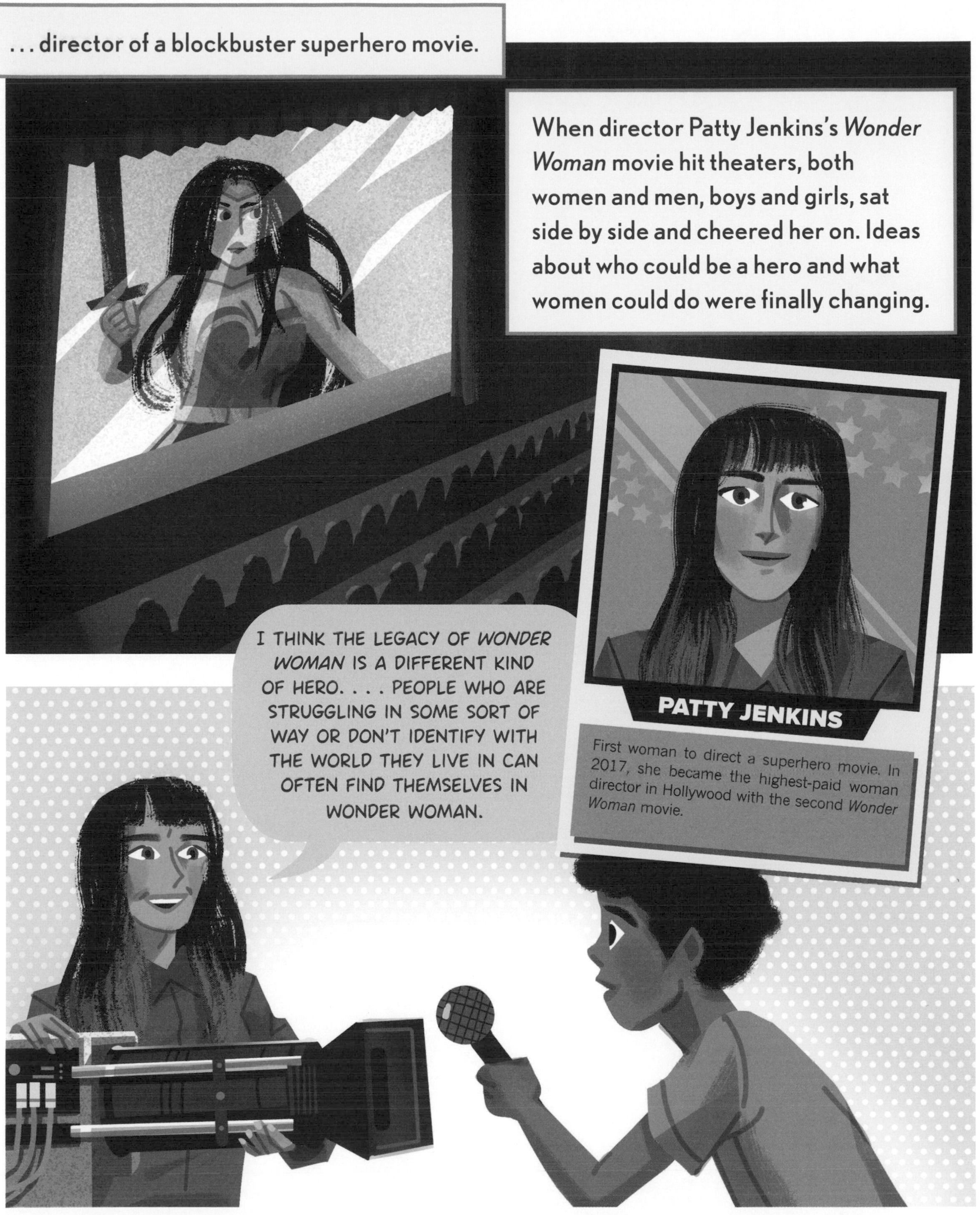

. . . director of a blockbuster superhero movie.
When director Patty Jenkins's *Wonder Woman* movie hit theaters, both women and men, boys and girls, sat side by side and cheered her on. Ideas about who could be a hero and what women could do were finally changing.
I THINK THE LEGACY OF *WONDER WOMAN* IS A DIFFERENT KIND OF HERO. . . . PEOPLE WHO ARE STRUGGLING IN SOME SORT OF WAY OR DON'T IDENTIFY WITH THE WORLD THEY LIVE IN CAN OFTEN FIND THEMSELVES IN WONDER WOMAN.
PATTY JENKINS
First woman to direct a superhero movie. In 2017, she became the highest-paid woman director in Hollywood with the second *Wonder Woman* movie.

For 80 years, Wonder Woman has changed people's minds. And in turn she's inspired us to change the world, making it a better place for all of us.

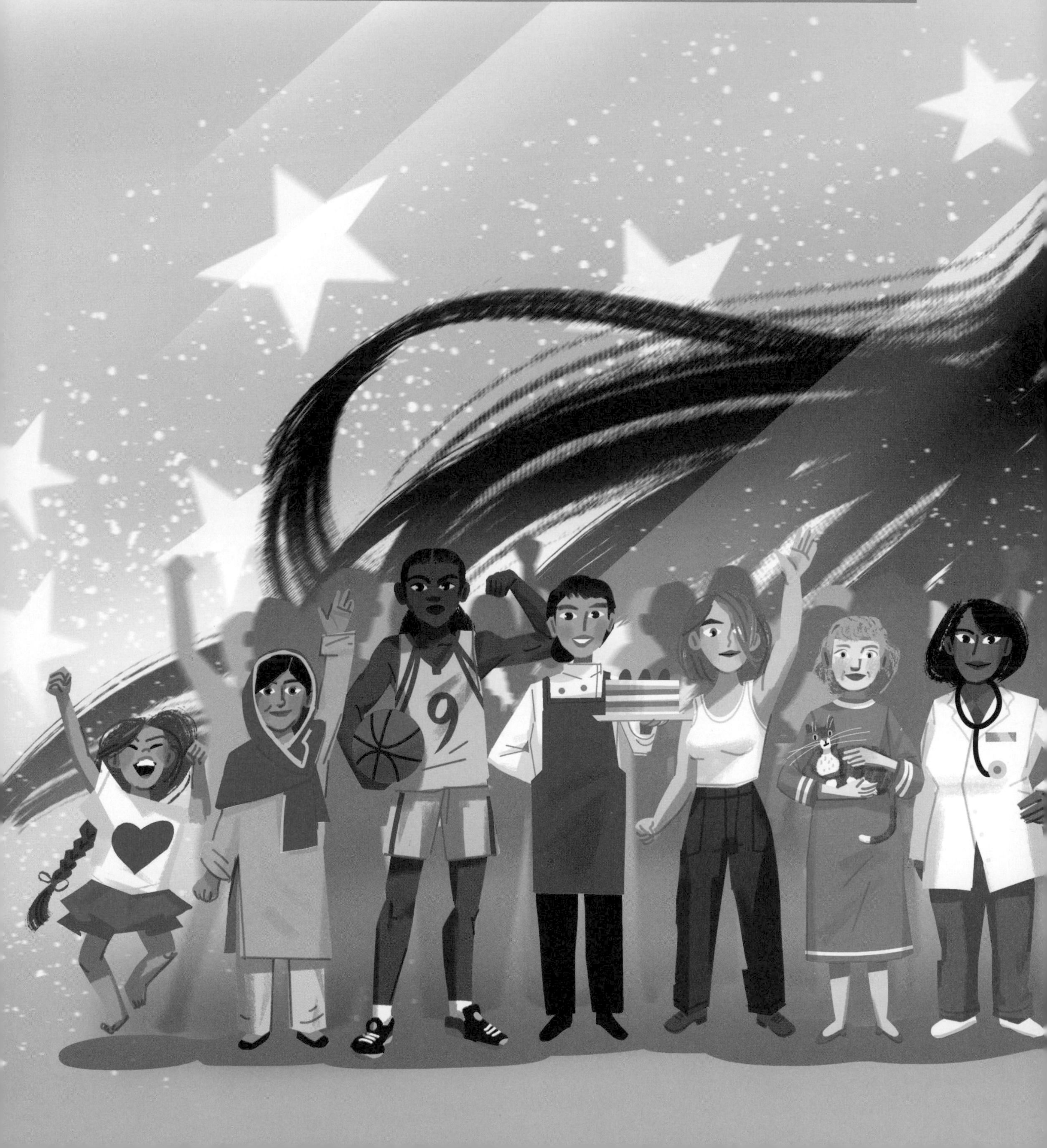

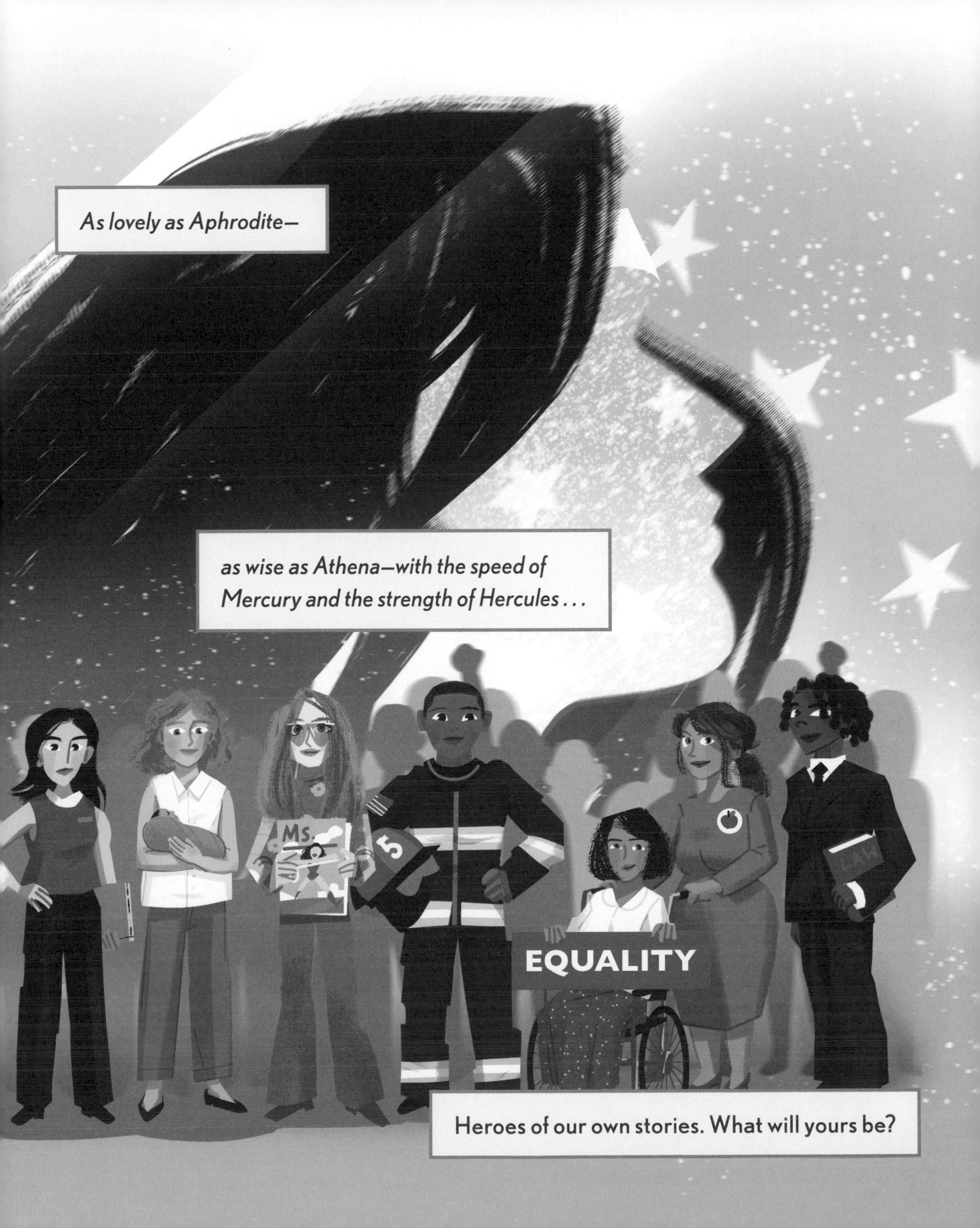
As lovely as Aphrodite—
as wise as Athena—with the speed of Mercury and the strength of Hercules . . .
Ms.
5
EQUALITY
Heroes of our own stories. What will yours be?

"'WONDER WOMAN' WAS CONCEIVED . . . TO SET UP A STANDARD AMONG CHILDREN AND YOUNG PEOPLE OF STRONG, FREE, COURAGEOUS WOMANHOOD; TO COMBAT THE IDEA THAT WOMEN ARE INFERIOR TO MEN; AND TO INSPIRE GIRLS TO SELF-CONFIDENCE AND ACHIEVEMENT IN ATHLETICS, OCCUPATIONS, AND PROFESSIONS MONOPOLIZED BY MEN."

–William Moulton Marston

THE ORIGIN STORY . . . OF THIS BOOK

As kids growing up in the 1970s, my sister and I weren't comic book readers, but we loved watching Lynda Carter as Wonder Woman on TV. We wore our Wonder Woman Underoos (a kind of underwear); made tiaras, lassos, and bracelets out of paper; and saved the world for hours. Wonder Woman has always been my favorite superhero.

When the movie came out in 2017, I sat beside my sister and sister-in-law, cheering Diana on as she battled the bad guys. And then I started asking myself those same questions that appeared in the introduction to each *Wonder Woman* comic. Who WAS she? Where DID she come from? And how did she become a symbol for strong and powerful women around the world?

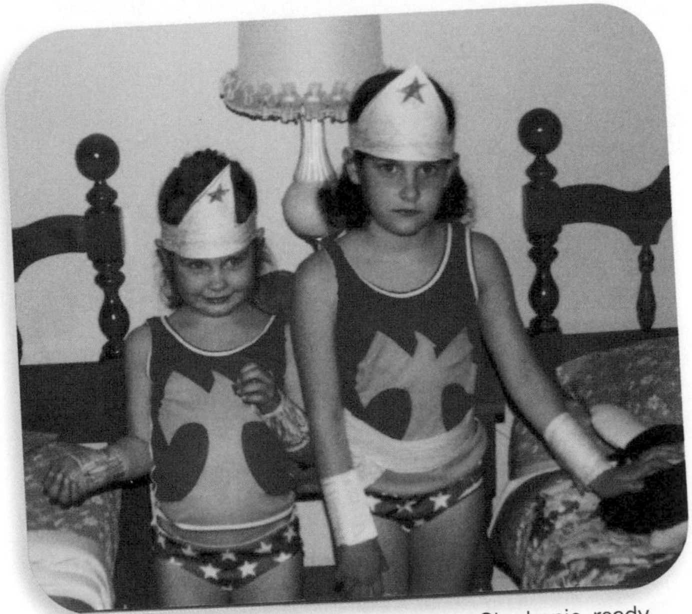

The author (right) at age six, and her sister, Stephanie, ready to battle evil in their Wonder Woman Underoos. Photo credit: Jennifer Williams

Looking for answers, I dug into Wonder Woman's history. I read biographies and comic book histories. I read old scripts and the early published comics. I visited archives at Brooklyn College and Harvard University to read letters from *Wonder Woman*'s editors, publishers, and writers from the Smithsonian Institution's Dibner Library collection. I watched the TV show and movie. And, in a major thrill, I talked with Joye Hummel who once wrote the stories herself in the 1940s.

For me, the idea of Wonder Woman is more important today than ever before. Though women have more freedom and equality in America than in the past, we still face many challenges to create a truly equal world. And women of color and other marginalized groups—who are missing from much of Wonder Woman's history—are still not widely represented in the comics, TV, or film industries. I hope we can look forward to a future that more fully represents and includes all women. So, as sisters, we put on our Wonder Woman T-shirts and leggings, and we fight for equality and justice for all women. Just like Wonder Woman's always done.

THE WOMEN OF *WONDER WOMAN*

In the early 1940s, the brand-new comic book industry was a man's world, even though some women worked as magazine illustrators and cartoonists for newspaper comic strips. Still, what surprised me as I researched *Wonder Woman* was how many women were involved in the comic in its early days. Aside from those mentioned in the story, the following women played a role.

Wonder Woman's looks, created by artist Harry G. Peter, may have been inspired by **Olive Richard**, who lived with Bill Marston's family, had dark hair, and wore signature cuff bracelets.

Lauretta Bender, MD, was a child psychiatrist. She became an official advisor to publisher Charlie Gaines and a champion for *Wonder Woman* and the benefits of comics for children. Bender reviewed each issue of *Wonder Woman*, suggested changes, and gave it a stamp of approval to ward off criticism.

Dorothy Roubicek Woolfolk was an assistant editor on *Wonder Woman*, beginning in 1942, and later the first woman editor at DC Comics. She worked closely with Lauretta Bender and the advisory board. But she may be best known for creating Kryptonite, Superman's weakness, while working on that comic book.

Marjorie Huntley worked as an inker and letterer under Harry Peter in the mid-1940s. An inker traced and shaded pencil-drawn images with ink so they copied well. Letterers handwrote all the text, while colorists colored the illustrations. Artists **Helen Schepens**, **Margaret Wroten**, and **Louise Marston** likely served as letterers and colorists on the comic.

Olive Richard, Lauretta Bender, and Marjorie Huntley

Dorothy Woodfolk

SOURCE NOTES

"As lovely as Aphrodite": Moulton, "Introducing Wonder Woman," 1.

"Come on, let's have a Superwoman!": "Elizabeth H. Marston," *New York Times.*

"The only hope for civilization": Marston, "Noted Psychologist Revealed."

"I picked *Superman*": Marston, "Why 100,000,000 Americans Read Comics."

"Why don't you": Marble and Leatherman, *Courting Danger,* 177.

"Wonder Woman symbolizes": Marston and Steinem, *Wonder Woman.*

"Wonder Woman is strong": Pace, "Lovely and Wise Heroine."

"It was a breakthrough": Smith, "*Wonder Woman*: Lynda Carter."

"I think the legacy of *Wonder Woman*": Setoodeh, "'Wonder Woman' Director."

"'Wonder Woman' was conceived": Marston, "Noted Psychologist Revealed."

SELECTED READING

Amazon Archives. www.amazonarchives.com.

Daniels, Les, and Chip Kidd. *Wonder Woman: The Complete History; The Life and Times of the Amazon Princess.* San Francisco: Chronicle Books, 2000.

Edgar, Joanne. "Wonder Woman Revisited." *Ms.,* July 1972, pp. 52–55. Found at the Internet Archive.

"Elizabeth H. Marston, Inspiration for Wonder Woman." *New York Times,* Apr. 3, 1993. www.nytimes.com/1993/04/03/obituaries/elizabeth-h-marston-inspiration-for-wonder-woman-100.html.

Hanley, Tim. *Wonder Woman Unbound: The Curious History of the World's Most Famous Heroine.* Chicago: Chicago Review Press, 2014.

Jones, Gerard. *Men of Tomorrow: Geeks, Gangsters, and the Birth of the Comic Book.* New York: Basic Books, 2004.

Lepore, Jill. *The Secret History of Wonder Woman.* New York: Vintage, 2015.

Marble, Alice, and Dale Leatherman. *Courting Danger.* New York: St. Martin's Press, 1991, p. 177.

Marston, William Moulton. "Noted Psychologist Revealed as Author of Best-Selling 'Wonder Woman' Children's Comic," press release, June 1942. Smithsonian Institution's Dibner Library.

—— "Why 100,000,000 Americans Read Comics." *American Scholar,* Jun. 8, 2017. theamericanscholar.org/wonder-woman. Originally published in *American Scholar,* Winter 1943–1944.

Marston, William Moulton, and Gloria Steinem. *Wonder Woman.* New York: Holt, Rinehart & Winston, 1972.

Moulton, Charles. "Introducing Wonder Woman." *All-Star Comics* #8. December 1941–January 1942, p. 1. Reprinted in Marston, William Moulton, and Gloria Steinem. *Wonder Woman.* New York: Holt, Rinehart & Winston, 1972.

Pace, Eric. "Lovely and Wise Heroine Summoned to Help with Feminist Cause." *New York Times,* Oct. 19, 1972.

Setoodeh, Ramin. "'Wonder Woman' Director Patty Jenkins on Equal Pay, Hollywood Sexism and James Cameron's Nasty Words." *Variety,* Oct. 10, 2017. variety.com/2017/film/features/patty-jenkins-wonder-woman-hollywood-sexism-equal-pay-james-cameron-1202583237.

Smith, Alyssa. "*Wonder Woman*: Lynda Carter on How Portraying the Original Warrior Princess Helped Shape a Generation." *Entertainment Weekly,* May 29, 2017. ew.com/movies/2017/05/29/wonder-woman-lynda-carter-original-portrayal-helped-shape-generation.

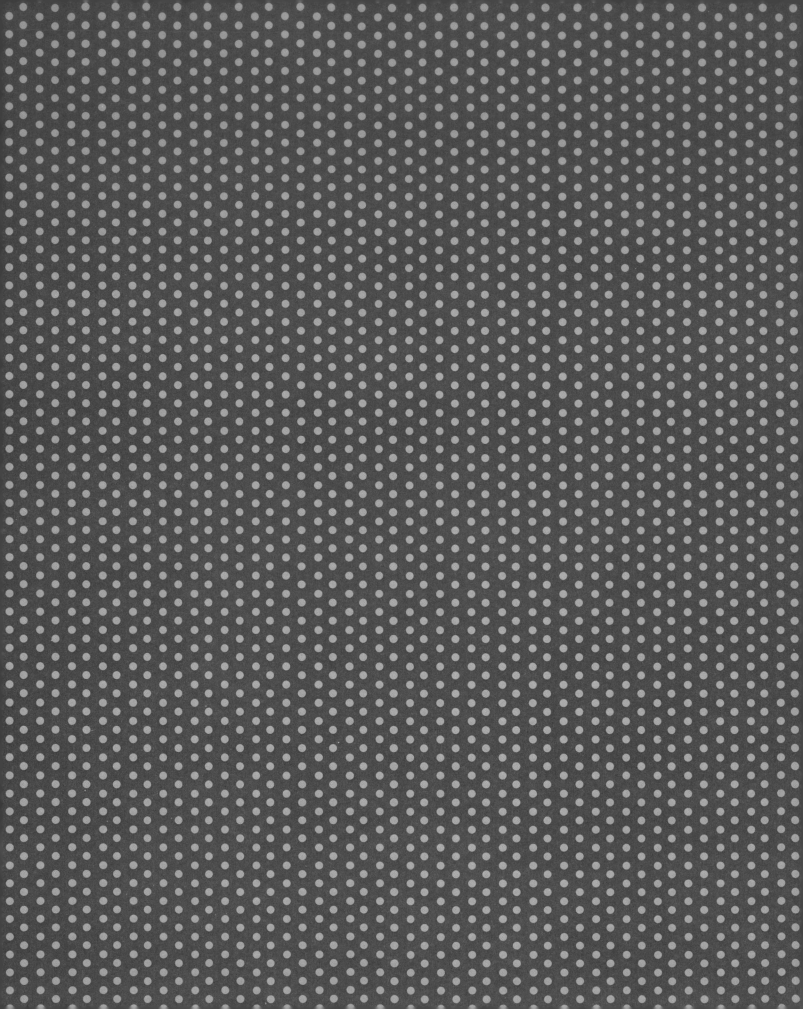